T0339567

Security Technology
Convergence Insights

Security Technology Convergence Insights

Ray Bernard

ELSEVIER

AMSTERDAM • BOSTON • HEIDELBERG • LONDON
NEW YORK • OXFORD • PARIS • SAN DIEGO
SAN FRANCISCO • SINGAPORE • SYDNEY • TOKYO

Security
Executive Council

Elsevier
Radarweg 29, PO Box 211, 1000 AE Amsterdam, Netherlands
The Boulevard, Langford Lane, Kidlington, Oxford OX5 1GB, UK
225 Wyman Street, Waltham, MA 02451, USA

Copyright © 2015 The Security Executive Council. Published by Elsevier Inc.
All rights reserved.

No part of this publication may be reproduced or transmitted in any form or by
any means, electronic or mechanical, including photocopying, recording, or any
information storage and retrieval system, without permission in writing from
the publisher. Details on how to seek permission, further information about the
Publisher's permissions policies and our arrangements with organizations such as the
Copyright Clearance Center and the Copyright Licensing Agency, can be found at our
website: www.elsevier.com/permissions.

Notices
Knowledge and best practice in this field are constantly changing. As new research and
experience broaden our understanding, changes in research methods, professional
practices, or medical treatment may become necessary.

Practitioners and researchers must always rely on their own experience and knowledge
in evaluating and using any information, methods, compounds, or experiments
described herein. In using such information or methods they should be mindful
of their own safety and the safety of others, including parties for whom they have a
professional responsibility.

To the fullest extent of the law, neither the Publisher nor the authors, contributors, or
editors, assume any liability for any injury and/or damage to persons or property as a
matter of products liability, negligence or otherwise, or from any use or operation of
any methods, products, instructions, or ideas contained in the material herein.

ISBN: 978-0-12-802842-1

British Library Cataloguing in Publication Data
A catalogue record for this book is available from the British Library

Library of Congress Cataloging-in-Publication Data
A catalog record for this book is available from the Library of Congress

For information on all Elsevier publications
visit our web site at store.elsevier.com/SecurityExecutiveCouncil

Working together
to grow libraries in
developing countries

www.elsevier.com • www.bookaid.org

Contents

Foreword

I have had the pleasure of knowing and respecting Ray Bernard for more than a decade. We first met when I attended my first security conference during the initial year of my own security consulting practice. In hindsight, I could not have been more fortunate. Ray was speaking about convergence at a SecureWorld Expo conference in Philadelphia, Pennsylvania. Our mutual interests coincided, and what followed was a series of long discussions from many different perspectives. Ray had been writing about convergence already in *Security Technology & Design* magazine (now *Security Technology Executive*), and I wrote a column about convergence in *Today's Security Integrator*. Little did we know how rapidly the pace of security convergence would accelerate and impact this industry.

In 2003 I established New Era Associates to specialize in the nascent field of security convergence. Having spent more than 20 years in executive sales roles within the information technology (IT) industry, I saw the need to integrate physical security solutions across IP networks to better share information and increase security efficiencies. This was early thinking for many in the physical security market; however, Ray Bernard is an innovative thinker, and he provided me the thought leadership, encouragement, and confidence I needed to believe that my instincts were correct. Eight years ago I was invited to join Brian T. Contos, William P. Crowell, Colby DeRodeff, and Dr. Eric Cole to collaborate on the book *Physical and Logical Security Convergence*, the first book published on the subject. We believed that security convergence would open many doors of opportunity for individuals in the physical security profession (CSOs, security directors, and security managers) and the physical security industry (manufacturers and technology service companies). That belief has proven true in a very big way.

When *Physical and Logical Security Convergence* was first published, there were few college or university courses on security, and none addressed security technology convergence. Today there are degree programs for physical security and IT security, and both programs include coverage of security convergence. In fact, some students will be reading this book as part of such a curriculum.

Security technology convergence refers to the union of physical security systems and information technology. The term itself has been around for more than a decade. Today nearly all electronic physical security systems are computer-based and reside on a network, which has led many security professionals to conclude that convergence has already happened and is now passé. Nothing could be further from the truth. This fine book, *Security Technology Convergence Insights*, chronicles security convergence from a number of perspectives. What you will gain from reading this book is a clear understanding of the lessons learned in more than a decade of deploying converged security systems, and you will come away a more informed security student or professional as a result.

Noted inventor and futurist Ray Kurzweil, in his 2012 book *How to Create a Mind*[1], reported his discovery that that if a technology is an information technology, the basic measures of price/performance and capacity follow amazingly precise exponential trajectories. Prices drop at an ever-increasing rate, and capabilities rise at an ever-increasing rate. These two information technology megatrends mean that the benefits of convergence grow increasingly greater every year.

If you deal with physical security technology, now is the time to get a full understanding of the current state of affairs regarding technology convergence in order to be better positioned to leverage the coming avalanche of technology advances in the field of security.

This book describes the subject of security convergence as a "broad-spectrum" issue and explains its impact on systems integration in detail, yet Ray Bernard also puts the subject matter into the context of clearly understandable real-world technology scenarios, outside the realm of the security industry. The continual acceleration of technical advances applied in the field of security and risk management will truly be astounding. Ray provides a roadmap to understanding this technical change and its impact on the security industry and its practitioners.

Looking back, Ray was a consistent advocate and sounding board for my own book and many articles, and I could depend on him for candid feedback and industry examples of cutting-edge security practices. He has spent his career at the forefront of security policy and technology innovation, and I cannot think of a better professional I would want to have a discussion with

---

[1]Ray Kurzweil, *How to Create a Mind: The Secret of Human Thought Revealed* (London: Viking Penguin. 2012) 255.

regarding the future of the security industry. The reader gets that privilege when opening this outstanding book. I am honored to endorse *Security Technology Convergence Insights*, an excellent work by my good friend and colleague, Ray Bernard.

Good reading,

Dan Dunkel
Co-author of *Physical and Logical Security Convergence*
Colleyville, TX

Preface

I consider myself fortunate that circumstances provided me with a wonderful path to security consulting that put me right in the center of security convergence early on. My technical work began in automotive body design, followed by education and then work in computers, networking, and software development. This path put me in an excellent position to understand the security technology convergence that started in the security industry in the 1970s (with the advent of computer-based access control and alarm systems) and with which I became involved in the late 1980s.

Security technology convergence refers to the incorporation of computing, networking, and communications technologies into electronic physical security systems. In the early days of security technology convergence the security industry was a cottage industry, and I think there were not more than 75 technology vendors at the international security conference that I attended in 1987. Nearly all of the vendors had a 10×10- or 10×20-ft booth, and signage was fairly minimal. This was 6 years after the introduction of the IBM personal computer, and not long after the term *computer phobia* made its appearance because so many people were finding personal computers to be daunting and intimidating. It was also 2 years before Lotus Notes email software was released, which sold 35,000 copies in the first year. Thus security technology convergence arrived to a physical security industry that was completely unprepared for it, was very slow in recognizing it, and was even slower in embracing it.

Today, of course, there are nearly 1000 vendors at that same security conference, most of whom are technology vendors. It's quite an extravaganza. And today, children grow up in an environment where computers and computerized devices and appliances are as ordinary as radio and television were in the 1980s. The very idea of computer phobia is almost laughable today.

Now consider the fact that the technological advances of the physical security industry have been enabled in large part by advances in computing and networking technologies—in other words, advances in information technology (or IT, as we more commonly refer to it). Today's security systems are IT systems. Thus two IT milestones significantly affected physical security systems. The first was the arrival of the personal computer in the 1980s. This helped fuel the adoption of card access control systems. The second was the adoption of enterprise-wide networking technologies, which organizations around the world welcomed in the early 2000s, partly in response to a need to replace their networking technology before the year 2000 (because of the Year 2000 Problem, commonly called the Y2K bug). The ability to place access control systems into a corporate network significantly reduced the cost of installation by allowing the lengthiest part of the access control wiring (from the main computer to the access control field panels) to be eliminated by sending the data over the corporate network. Corporate networking made enterprise-wide access control systems feasible and more affordable.

Other technological trends were also in play at the time, such as the ability to update firmware (software on computer chips) over the network, instead of having to send a technician to physically replace one or more computer chips. As the pace of IT advances continued to accelerate, the physical security industry continued to lag behind IT advances by at least 2–3 years.

This is the context for security technology convergence and what led me to begin writing about it in 2006 in a column titled "Convergence Q&A" published in *Security Technology & Design* magazine. Along the way the magazine's name changed to *Security Technology Executive*—but no distinction concerning the name under which the chapter material was published is made here.

This book is a compilation of material from my Convergence Q&A column, which originally started with answers provided by readers to the questions that I posed in each magazine issue. After a while, readers reversed the situation and began submitting questions to me. As time went forward, fewer and fewer readers submitted answers and more and more readers submitted questions. Additional questions came from attendees at security conferences where I spoke during individual sessions and panel discussions, as well as from attendees of the ASIS International workshops in which I participated as part of the workshop faculty. When I couldn't answer the questions immediately based on my own experience or that of my colleagues, I searched them out.

Thus the Q&A format varies throughout, with some answers being provided by readers and some answers being provided by me as the writer of the column. Some answers are brief, followed by a closer look at the issues involved. Some questions required the entire column to answer fully. This explains the variations in style between the various sections of this book, even within a single chapter.

These questions and answers come from an 8-year period that constitutes, in my opinion, the greatest time of technological change to date for the physical security industry. This is by no means the end of the story, for the pace of technological changes continues to increase, and there will be many more lessons to be learned going forward. The material in this book should provide an excellent start by presenting the hard-won lessons of convergence during the period of the most significant technical advances in the industry so far.

Acknowledgments

First and foremost, my heartfelt thanks go to my wife and business partner, Pamela Peak, who is a writer and editor of award-winning documentary films as well as screen and stage plays. It was she who first encouraged me to begin writing for security journals and magazines over 20 years ago, and she has always been an understanding sounding board when I faced one writing challenge or another.

Next, boundless thanks go to three people who have been editors for my columns and articles at *Security Technology Executive* magazine (formerly *Security Technology & Design*) over the past 20 years: Steve Lasky, currently Editorial Director for Cygnus Security Media Group, publisher of *Security Technology Executive*; Marleah Blades, formerly Managing Editor at Cygnus Business Media; and Paul Rothman, currently Editor in Chief, *Security Dealer & Integrator* magazine for Cygnus Business Media. In addition, over the past decade I have had more discussions about security convergence with Steve Lasky than I have with any other individual. In 2003, when I first proposed a series of articles about security convergence to Steve, I found him to have great insight into the subject and to be as passionate about it as I was.

This book would not have happened without the strong encouragement and support of Bob Hayes, Managing Director of the Security Executive Council. I met Bob in 2004 when we both participated at a SecureWorld Expo panel discussion, and we had a "meeting of the minds" on a number of security topics. Since then Bob has shared with me many insights relating to security management convergence and has kept me up to speed on the leading thinking on the topic of a converged business security risk perspective, with regard to both the theory and the practice involved.

Great thanks go also to James Connor, Principal/CEO of N2N Secure and former Senior Manager of Global Security Systems for Symantec. James and I spent many Saturday morning hours and countless other times discussing convergence from numerous perspectives from 2006 through 2008. I have encountered no one before or since who could articulate the many aspects of security convergence as accurately or effectively as James can. I don't know of any who has given as much of his personal time to share those understandings with as many security practitioners as James has.

I am also truly grateful for the shared experiences and insights from my many colleagues on the ASIS International Physical Security Council and IT Security Council, who are all top thinkers in their own fields of practice and who have given me valuable perspectives on the various aspects of security convergence.

About the Author

Ray Bernard is a security consultant and author who has provided pivotal direction and advice in the security industry and the security profession for over 26 years. Ray is President and Principal Consultant of Ray Bernard Consulting Services (www.go-rbcs.com), a group of highly expert corporate, physical, and IT security consultants with outstanding track records in their fields of expertise. Ray has led many noteworthy security projects for international airports, nuclear disarmament facilities, sports stadiums, water districts, manufacturing plants, multiple-tower high-rise facilities, and corporate headquarters facilities.

Ray is also the convergence editor for *Security Technology Executive* magazine (formerly *Security Technology & Design*), for which he writes the "Convergence Q&A" column as well as highly regarded articles about key security topics. He was named one of security's *Top 10 Movers and Shakers* of 2006 by *Security Technology & Design* magazine.

Ray is a physical security professional, a designation awarded by ASIS International, of which he is an active member. Ray sits on the educational committees of both the Physical Security Council and the IT Security Council. Ray is also board-certified in Homeland Security (CHS-III) by the American Board for Certification in Homeland Security of the American College of Forensic Examiners Institute.

Ray is a contributing author to the *Encyclopedia of Security Management, Second Edition* (2007), covering the topics of the convergence of physical security and IT; access control levels; and authentication, authorization, and cryptography.

Introduction

There was a strong inclination to rewrite all of this book's material into an educational text on the subject of technology convergence. After a little bit of work along that line, several things became evident. First, each piece of information would no longer be available in a quickly digestible "snippet" tied to a real event or experience of someone dealing with a particular aspect of convergence. That would make the material less readable, not something that could be picked up in a free moment and used to quickly advance one's knowledge or understanding of security convergence in a worthwhile way. Second, by blending each piece in with other information, the real-life flavor and context would be lost. Instead of shared experience, it would become shared ideas. The "lessons learned" aspect would disappear. Finally, by making an academic presentation of the subject matter, the level of effort required to grasp the material fully would be increased. It would require study and concentration, not just quick reading.

Instead, the task became one of organizing the related material into subject groupings, with each grouping then becoming a chapter. This turned out to be a challenge because many of the topics were related to more than one other topic.

So, while the chapter categories were developed based on what seemed to be the best fit among a number of choices, it is important to state here, at the outset, that reading this book in chapter order is only one way to approach the material. The particular topic that relates more strongly to your plans and your experience will vary from reader to reader. Scanning the various topics and then starting to read those that seem to be of most interest to you or of greatest relevance to your immediate responsibilities may be more beneficial.

There is one final important introductory note. If you find that you have questions that are not answered in the book, or you realize you have answers that you don't see in the book and that you'd like to share, please send me an email note at ConvergenceQA@go-rbcs.com. I'll respond to you directly and, with your permission, may very well include them in an upcoming Convergence Q&A column, either anonymously or with attribution to you, however you wish. I'm a big fan of sharing knowledge and I hope that you are, too.

Ray Bernard

CHAPTER 1

What Is Security Convergence?

Convergence is commonly defined as two or more distinct or separate things coming together. It is often used with things that flow, such as water, air currents, and vehicle or pedestrian traffic. After all, if things are not moving, how can they come together? The term applies, for example, when two lanes of vehicle traffic converge into a single lane.

However, *convergence* is also a technical term used by designers and engineers. Vehicle drivers don't use or think about the word *convergence*, even though when driving they focus very closely on the specific point of convergence—the point where the traffic comes together. The drivers who accomplish the convergence are those who point their vehicles in the correct direction and adjust vehicle speed accordingly. Interestingly enough, drivers don't use the word *convergence*. Drivers focus on convergence as a secondary concern. *Their primary concern is getting to their destination safely and quickly.* That they may have to merge their vehicle into a different flow of traffic to change freeways is just another aspect of driving, and it doesn't require new vocabulary words like *convergence*.

Similarly, when performing their security jobs, end users of security technology or security management systems don't use the term *convergence*. They just use the vocabulary of the jobs they are doing. Most security practitioners, however, do need to understand security convergence, even if they won't use the word much, because it affects how they design security technology systems and how they develop and improve their security management systems. Security convergence is currently ongoing and will be for at least the next decade, which means that in one way or another it will impact the majority of security practitioners.

TWO TYPES OF CONVERGENCE

Security convergence refers to the convergence of historically distinct aspects of security. There are two types of security convergence: security technology convergence and security management convergence.

Security technology convergence refers to the incorporation of information technology (IT) into electronic physical security systems. Today, security systems are built using IT components such as computers, software, databases, and networks that are, for the most part, based on standards. Security systems have been made more affordable and reliable by the use of common business computing and networking technologies. Electronic physical security systems previously were built using proprietary technologies that stood alone and were not interconnected with other systems or networks. Today, as communications, computing, and other digital technologies continue to advance, their new capabilities will be adopted into security systems and products by the security industry. Thus, as business and consumer technologies continue to be adopted for security use, security technology convergence will continue to occur well into the next decade and beyond.

Security management convergence refers to the bringing together of previously distinct corporate security, physical security, and IT security functions under a single point of management, which could be an individual management position such as a Chief Security Officer or a committee or council such as an Enterprise Risk Council. The Security Executive Council has coined the term *unified risk oversight*™ for the resulting unified risk perspective. Rarely will the new perspective be called "converged security" because more appropriate terms such as "unified risk management" will be adopted. In the long term, once the unified perspectives become commonplace rather than the exception, the word "unified" will probably be dropped in favor of the simpler phrase "risk management," whose meaning then will have evolved to encompass a broader scope.

SECURITY CONVERGENCE COLLABORATION

As mentioned above, there are two types of security convergence: security technology convergence and security management convergence. Thus there are two areas of convergence collaboration. For example, between physical security and IT functions there is one scope of collaboration at the management level to address security risk management and another scope of collaboration at the operations level to address the IT aspects of electronic physical security systems.

Although this book deals mostly with technology convergence, there is also some mention of management convergence, which will be easily recognizable even it if is not specifically called out as such.

THE INTRODUCTION OF THE TERM "CONVERGENCE"

Individuals who have recently entered the field of security, either in the course of formal education or by accepting a security position, have been introduced to many of the results of convergence often without the term *convergence* ever being used in the discussion. That's because once two separate things have converged, they are now referred to by an appropriately descriptive name for their converged state. Discussions about them don't need to use the word *convergence*.

On the other hand, security practitioners who entered the security field before or during the 1990s most likely have encountered the term *convergence* as it was first used by security industry marketers. Many of the marketers and sales people apparently did not fully understand what security technology convergence was. At that time there was a lot of confusion and "mental fog" about convergence. Most people in the security industry (manufacturers and service providers) thought that convergence simply meant putting security systems onto an Internet protocol (IP) network and using network-connected servers and workstations. That thinking brought many in the security industry to declare that security technology convergence was "over," starting around 2010. To them it was something that had happened and was now old news, even though security technology convergence is still ongoing.

Regardless of when you were first introduced to security convergence, the material in this chapter and those that follow provide you with insight into the evolution of thinking on the subject of security convergence and lessons learned along the way.

FOUR CATEGORIES OF CONVERGENCE

Security convergence is a broad spectrum, which I break down into four categories:

- *Convergence of electronic security systems and IT:* This started back in the 1980s with the introduction of the personal computer and kept advancing as computer, network, and information system technologies advanced. It includes all of the "IP" convergence phenomena. It means, among other things, that physical security professionals need to be more IT-savvy.
- *Internetworking of physical security and business systems and networks:* This, too, has been going on since the 1980s and even earlier, when access control systems first started being used for tracking time and attendance. Now it's really taking off: security video systems are being used for quality, safety, training, and supervision, as well as for security surveillance.
- *Integration of physical and IT security systems:* This is the realm of one-card initiatives and connecting physical access control with information system access control. A common example cited is to ensure that you cannot log on to a computer if you haven't used your security card or

biometric print to gain access into the room the computer is in, thus preventing someone else from using your login credentials in your absence.

- *Integration of physical and IT security management:* Also known as holistic security, integrated security management, and, more recently, enterprise security risk management, this is the adoption of a unified risk perspective for managing security at senior executive levels.

What defines these categories is that they each have a different set of security stakeholders. They also tend to have their own unique security challenges, which is the subject of the question below. The answer to the first question posed below lists the top five convergence challenges that my column readers and security conference attendees submitted, starting with the most frequently submitted.

Dave Tyson, author of *Security Convergence: Managing Enterprise Security Risk,* discusses two types of security convergence: technology convergence and management convergence. The first two categories above fall under technology convergence. The third category involves a little of both, and the last category is all about security management convergence.

Shayne Bates, a leading security strategist, advisor, and advocate, coined the term *convergence engineering* to label the technical work involved in the first three convergence categories. This helps those working in the field identify themselves as individuals who possess the knowledge and experience needed to successfully address technical convergence issues.

Q: What aspect of convergence do you find most challenging?

A:

1. Figuring out how "convergence technology" will impact my existing systems, which for the most part are working okay and do not need replacement, but which are not the same brands and are not global like our IT systems are.
2. Trying to determine if I should expand my video system using the kind of components I have already, or if I should start moving over to network cameras and network video recorders (NVRs) instead of DVRs.
3. How to deal with the fact that my systems integrator doesn't seem to be up to speed on IT issues and does not seem comfortable talking about network based security technology with my IT department personnel.
4. Explaining to management what security convergence is about.
5. Finding the right person in IT to collaborate with in regards to convergence.

MASTERING CONVERGENCE

Although the term *convergence* has been written about, presented, and discussed for years, many security practitioners still do not have complete answers to these two questions: How do you go from security strategy, to tactics, to security operations and take convergence into account? Where does technology start to fit into the picture?

In spite of the lack of clarity around the term *convergence*, security practitioners have been working to apply what they know to form a concept of convergence that relates to their own organizations. It should be no surprise that their thoughts and opinions gravitate toward the organizational perspective.

Q: What is your current concept of convergence, based on your own experience with it?

A: As a security professional since 1989 and in management for the past 15 years, a wise security manager learns everything from human behaviour, business processes and technology, or the elements of any systems. I started off as a typical security manager focused on the operations, the backbone of any security service without a doubt. However, moving on to the corporate world, the challenges become significant and complex. I can't say I'm an expert on anything but I'm a pretty good generalist who has a good base knowledge that relates to the corporate world (finances, HR, health & safety, legal, facilities & property, IT, insurance and the likes).

Convergence for me is like "intelligence:" "foreseeability," "adaptability" and "capability." A manager, like a commander, masters his environment to achieve the mission.

—**Paul H. Aubé, B.Sc., CPP, Corporate Security Manager, Groupe TVA, Inc., Montreal, Canada.**

A: In my opinion, one of the primary difficulties associated with achieving a higher level of convergence is the low level of interaction between the physical and IT teams with regard to the risk management aspect of security. Furthermore, one can tend to perceive the other as having a hidden agenda, which in many cases could be easily resolved through a willingness to communicate and simply do what is best for the organization. It is easy to focus on technology issues, because they are concrete and specific. However, it is increasingly difficult to focus on organizational and risk issues, but that's where the key ingredient to successful convergence and the benefits to be gained lie.

— **Frank A. Cirillo, Director, Security & Facilities, Syracuse Research Corporation, North Syracuse, New York, USA.**

INTEGRATION OF PHYSICAL SECURITY AND LOGICAL SECURITY

One aspect of convergence is the integration of physical security and logical security. This is happening at two levels: security technology and security management. One example of security technology integration is one-step provisioning, where physical and logical access privileges are assigned in a single step. Another is the integration of physical and logical access control authorization, where, for instance, you cannot log on to a computer in a room that you haven't physically entered using card access. Integration at the security technology level requires, to some extent, integration at the security management level. At a minimum, establishing how the physical and logical systems interact with each other is required.

Security management integration starts with having a unified risk perspective, which is why the term "enterprise security risk management" was coined. Enterprise security risk management also has been described as converging security with the enterprise because the starting point for security practitioners is learning all about the business functions of the enterprise. If you don't know what each business function does, how can you understand what its security risks are? Thus many security practitioners have begun the process of learning more about each function of their organization, with extremely positive results.

Q: How has learning about your organization's business functions affected your work?

A: It has caused a 180 degree shift in the attitudes towards security. Previously I was perceived by other managers as forwarding Security's agenda; now I am perceived as supporting the various departmental agendas. Previously, most of my interaction concerned security violations or security incidents. Now, most of my interaction concerns security risks, security planning, and how to protect critical business processes. That makes me an ally of all of our managers. More recently on a one-on-one basis I brought up the subject of business continuity with each department's managers, explaining what that would mean for the critical functions of each department. At a corporate meeting they voted unanimously to establish a business continuity steering committee to oversee the updating of our Y2K-era BCP plan. A year ago it would have been like pulling teeth to get even token participation. A few supervisors have also asked about the possibility of deploying additional security cameras in their area for supervisory purposes. I and my senior security staff really feel like—and are—integral parts of the business planning process. Not only does Security have more visibility at management levels, but the business security risks are much more visible to us as well.

—Security Manager, Major Manufacturing Company.

A: I really think I understand more about each of our business functions now than our CEO does. I'm not kidding about that. I never talked about security—I framed all the conversations around risk. That's something that business managers can wrap their wits around. It was easy to get the conversations rolling, and I learned a lot about how we could better deploy our security technology, and improve our security processes and procedures. I also learned what I needed to be able to document the cost–benefit aspects of our planned security improvements.

—Director of Global Security, Major Pharmaceutical Company.

A: Once I started presenting my security proposals within the context of risk mitigation and risk management, I have not had a single security initiative turned down in over 4 years. Previous to that, even after September 11th, I didn't have that track record.

—Director of Global Security, Major Software Company.

WHY CONVERGENCE DIDN'T REALLY DISAPPEAR

At the Global Security Operations 2010 event at the RAND Corporation, one of the attendees provided a very insightful answer to this discussion question:

Q: What bugs you most about convergence?

A: What really bugs me about convergence is that people keep talking about physical security and IT security being separate. They make statements to the effect that physical security and IT don't get along, how different their cultures are, and so on. There is too much focus on what's separate, and that goes in the opposite direction of convergence, which is that things come together. I work in IT, but I have a strong background in physical security. I see physical and IT security having a lot in common but I don't see people focusing on that. To a certain extent I think the common focus on *differences* is counter-productive.

—Chuck Hutchings, IT Manager, Dynamic Air Engineering (www.dynamic-air.com).

Chuck's comments place him about 2 years ahead of the current state of physical security and IT technology convergence, if the physical security industry follows the path of the IT industry.

Convergence "Disappears" in the IT Domain

Starting in 2003 I began tracking the Google® search results for three words: *convergence information technology*. The graph shows the trend of webpages containing those three words, and I have presented this graph annually at a number of security conferences since 2003.

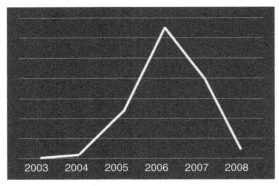

When	# Web Pages
April 2003	650,000
June 2004	1,430,000
Sept 2005	24,600,000
July 2006	65,100,000
July 2007	39,900,000
Sept 2008	1,780,000

Webpages containing the words *convergence information technology* between 2003 and 2008.

The number of websites reached its peak in July 2006, with over 26 million pages containing the three convergence key words. It continued dropping in 2007 and 2008. What does this up-and-down trend represent? In 2007 I mistakenly thought that the peak represented a marketing "hype factor" present in 2006 and that the drop in 2007 represented the disappearance of marketing hype around convergence and "getting down to business." A cursory examination of some of the search results tended to indicate this. The further decrease in 2008 stood to refute that hypothesis, so a closer examination was in order. I was able to use the Internet Archive's Wayback Machine (www.archive.org) to look at some of the older pages. (The Internet Archive contains 85 billion webpages archived from 1996 to a few months ago.)

Closer analysis revealed the graph showed not a "hype factor" effect but the result of convergence actually taking place. Convergence in the IT domain is basically *voice, data, and video being transmitted over the same cable*. Variations of that definition, once common on the Internet, now appear on few pages—less than 125,000 as this work is being written. What does this mean?

As convergence was taking place, discussions about it were being replaced by discussions about the solutions that resulted: voice over IP, power over Ethernet, IP telephones, streaming video, and so on. The resulting applications—which use the converged technologies—are more affordable, more convenient, and more powerful than previous applications as a result of using common standards and common communications infrastructures and having a very high degree of interoperability. For example, compare the iPhone® with any preconvergence telephone, mobile, or wired.

The results of convergence in the IT world provide two important messages for the physical security industry and the security profession that it serves:

- *Technical knowledge* about convergence remains important for those who build and install systems, but will become less and less important for those who operate them.
- Security managers, as well as system operators, need *applications knowledge*, which is where the value of converged technologies impact security operations and enable improved risk mitigation. Knowledge of security applications will become the primary domain of security technology leadership.

CHAPTER 2

Convergence Trends

Now that physical security systems are basically Information Technology (IT) systems in terms of their technology, the trends that affect computing, electronic data, and electronic communications also impact the design and use of physical security systems. Another type of convergence that impacts the deployment of physical security systems is occurring—the convergence of virtual modeling (computer-based modeling) with building construction industry practice. Instead of creating physical models of buildings, architects and engineers are creating computer-based virtual models.

To most easily take maximum advantage of convergence opportunities requires knowledge of the various trends involved, and the impacts of some of the convergence-related trends are presented in this chapter.

THE VALUE OF TECHNOLOGY

After each year's ASIS Annual Seminars and Exhibits conference, I usually write about the technology that affects convergence in one way or another. One time, however, the conference prompted a different response—not about technology products or features, but about technology value.

Q: What did you see in the ASIS exhibit hall of value?

A: I am invariably asked the question each year. Before addressing what's new and valuable in technology, it is worth considering how exactly the word "value" should be applied. What prompts me to give thought to this is that three manufacturers made statements in writing or verbally during the show to the effect that "it is all about partnerships," referring to their partnerships with other companies.

In some cases the partnerships are with competitors, and I give the companies involved great credit for embracing "coopetition," a term coined in the 1980s by Novell's founder Ray Noorda. The essence of "coopetition" is that you cooperate with others to increase the size of the market, and then compete with those same others for your share of the expanded market. The idea is that everyone will fare better by having a larger market to divide up (see "Coopetition Arrives," *Security Technology & Design*, October 2005, available online at: http://www.securityinfowatch.com/article/10520467/coopetition-arrives). Markets can be expanded in a number of ways, but one of them is to offer something that's of greater value to customers than what has been previously available.

Coopetition and Open Standards

In the case of the security industry, open standards are one means of offering greater value. By increasing the interoperability among products and systems, customers can select products and systems (or various parts of them) that are the best fit for their needs, creating an overall system that has more value to the customer than a single brand's offering. In particular, this solves a problem relating to video management system (VMS) software and cameras: The proprietary interfaces required for each camera brand have made supporting a wide variety of camera brands an extreme burden for VMS development. Money that could otherwise go into features of value for the customer has gone to supporting interfaces to cameras, and as cameras continue to advance, the developmental burden never stops. This has limited the value provided to customers each year.

Thus I was heartened by recent demonstrations from the Physical Security Interoperability Alliance and the Open Network Video Interface Forum for two reasons: first, the demonstrations worked; second, the member companies kept to their previously announced development schedules. This shows that the companies are truly taking their commitments seriously.

Technological Value

The value of any security technology lies in how it enables security practitioners to do one or more of the following:

- *Increase security effectiveness* (reduce risk).
- *Increase security efficiency* (reduce costs and/or increase productivity).
- *Add value to the business* (such as how video cameras and video analytics can be used for nonsecurity business purposes).

For one product to be "better" than another product requires more than having a longer feature list or bigger numbers on a data sheet. The issue is decided by whether the product's features, data sheet numbers, and cost provide more value according to the three criteria listed above. *Thus value is relative to the customer, to the customer's existing and future technology deployments, to the potential improvements to the risk picture, and to the potential business value to the customer's organization.* The world's most impressive Pan-Tilt-Zoom (PTZ) camera is of no value if there are no security operations personnel who operate it. Value is relative to each customer's situation, and many customers in the same business sector, such as retail stores, have some needs and requirements in common.

The general principle is somewhat obvious but can still get lost in all the marketing language about "channels," "distribution," "partnerships," and so on. During the ASIS conference I heard the word "customer" much less frequently than I did these other terms.

Ultimately, it's all about the customer and the value that the customer can provide to his or her organization by utilizing the products and services being offered. Even customers can sometimes lose sight of that in the quest to identify the "best technology." The best product in any technology category is the one that will do the best job increasing security effectiveness and operations efficiency and adding value to the business.

THE SECURITY INDUSTRY WORLD HAS CHANGED

The security industry now functions in a new world—*one where companies that release networked products and systems that are not ready for safe deployment find that their customers quickly become aware of it.* Here is a question I received from a security practitioner who approached his IT department about putting security systems onto the corporate network to achieve a number of important benefits.

> **Q: I told IT that I wanted to put two of our security systems onto the corporate network. They asked me for vendor names, software and firmware version numbers and release notes, and vulnerability disclosures. What is a vulnerability disclosure, and why are they asking for it?**
>
> **A:** Vulnerability disclosure is (a) the practice of publishing information (disclosures) about a computer security problem, and (b) a type of policy that specifies guidelines for doing so. Disclosure may be published by the person or organization that discovers the vulnerability, or by a responsible body such as the Computer Emergency Response Team (CERT). Sometimes the vendor is alerted prior to disclosure, and is allowed a certain amount of time to fix the problem before the vulnerability information is published. CERT's *Vulnerability Disclosure Policy* can be read here: http://www.cert.org/vulnerability-analysis/vul-disclosure.cfm.

IT teams ask for vulnerability disclosures because they are responsible for seeing that all systems and devices are deployed securely on their network. They need information to do this. In the absence of such information, a researcher may be tasked with collecting information and identifying vulnerabilities, including by directly examining the products or systems. Direct examinations are becoming more commonplace.

Video System Attack

In 2009 at the DEFCON conference, which describes itself as "the hacker community's foremost social network," a network research firm (people who do network penetration testing for a living) hacked a brand-name system and fed copied video back into its video display and recording stream. They picked up an object off a table, but the video system showed the object as still being there. This type of attack is called a "replay attack," where data recorded earlier is played back later and fed into the system.

A sophisticated version of this attack would involve injecting captured video data of the object's removal several hours later than when it actually occurred. The system's time-stamped video would then provide "evidence" of the object's removal at a time when the attackers were several "hours away" establishing a solid alibi. The recorded video would be properly watermarked by video management software, thus falsely "authenticating" the fact that the attackers "couldn't have done it."

You can access the 50-minute video of their presentation from the Bp.IP website (www.bpforip.com/news/video-surveillance-system-hacked). The video shows the demonstration, the Cisco camera model, and the technical points of how it was done. (Note that the network research firm stated that before the conference, they provided a proposed solution to Cisco and were working with them on the technical details.)

Access Control System Attack

In 2010 at CarolinaCon, an annual hacker's conference in North Carolina, security researcher Shawn Merdinger presented his successful attack on a brand-name networked access control system. He commented during the presentation that "The problem is that they [facilities and physical security] have this convergence … and they are slapping this stuff onto your network. So you need to be aware of what's going on." Not only does he demonstrate how easy it was to hack the access control system, he puts the company's marketing statements about how safe it is to connect the system to the Internet up on the screen. He then demonstrates an Internet search that locates many such systems that are connected to the Internet and wide open to the type of hack he demonstrates. Like any good security researcher, Shawn reported the vulnerabilities to the CERT Coordination Center (CERT/CC) and worked with them to follow responsible disclosure practices. He also outlined steps to mitigate their impact.

You can view the 57-minute video of his presentation and see the slides from his talk at: www.bpforip.com/news/access-control-system-hacked.

The New World

In the IT world, vulnerabilities are hunted and found as a matter of normal daily business by network research firms whose role it is to find vulnerabilities so that they can be fixed. They also perform penetration testing for their customers, who require verification that their own systems are being maintained at an acceptable level of security.

From now on, *it will be the rule rather than the exception* that hacker conferences include one or more sessions about how to hack physical security systems—just as they contain sessions about hacking telephones, web servers, information systems, and so on.

Whether you are a manufacturer, a consultant, a systems integrator, or an end-user customer, it is now critical that you begin paying attention to the vulnerabilities of the products and systems you provide or depend on.

Q: How did Shawn Merdinger come to investigate the particular access control system?

A: His company was thinking of purchasing one. He was simply doing his job as an IT professional—ensuring that his company would not put itself at risk by installing a vulnerable product or system.

In a recent discussion with a product manager and a sales manager from one security industry manufacturing company, the product manager stated that he didn't think this kind of IT evaluation was very common. "None of our customers have mentioned this to us," he said. "You may be making more out of this than the situation warrants." I explained that in 100% of my global company clients the IT department evaluates all systems and devices that will connect to the network, including physical security systems and devices. I also informed him that I doubted his products would pass such an evaluation because (a) the user manual shipped didn't fully match the product; (b) there was no installation guide (the company expected all installations to be performed by factory-trained installers); (c) the software user interface did not follow the Microsoft Windows user interface guidelines (a significant defect in a 3-year-old product); and (d) the online help was incomplete and inconsistent from window to window in the application. (Unfortunately, these shortcomings are common to many industry products.)

I doubted that any of this company's customers performed IT evaluations, or they would not be customers! They would have selected a more qualified product from an IT perspective. Even in those cases where IT is not involved in product evaluation, however, successfully selling a less-qualified product can reduce customer status (the status of the security manager from the perspective of IT) when IT finds a product on the network that doesn't meet IT's standards or isn't developed to professional standards.

Defensive attitudes on the part of manufacturers astound me because they are backward thinking. *Who wouldn't want to have software that is very easy to use because it follows Microsoft Windows conventions?* (I know there are Windows vs.

Mac arguments on usability, so don't miss my point: Regardless of the operating system, the software should have very high usability for first-time users.) *Who wouldn't want to have a product that IT departments embrace because it is professionally developed and packaged and can be easily evaluated? Who wouldn't want their security practitioner customers to impress IT by selecting a top-notch product?* Furthermore, what IT department wouldn't be pleased to have a "hardening guide" booklet or chapter in the product or system installation instructional material? Since there are no clear leaders in this area, any company with a sound product could take a leading position.

Right now, security practitioners can't go wrong assuming that all physical security systems are vulnerable as shipped from the factory. I was about to write that I know of no commercial off-the-shelf system that ships with specific instructions for secure network deployment or system hardening. Then I learned from my network research colleague Rodney Thayer that Firetide (www.firetide.com) does include hardening information in one of its installation documents—but it is buried in the midst of other things as opposed to highlighted front and center, as the industry needs.

The good news is that this picture is starting to change.

IP-Based Card Readers Compromised

Network researchers Michael Gough and Ian Robertson recently made a video for the BSides regional security event that took place in Austin, Texas, in March 2011. The video chronicled how they easily unlocked the reader-controlled doors at an association swimming pool using a small application written for an Android phone.

The targeted access control system was one that is remotely managed via the Internet, which is how they accessed it. But the system would have been just as vulnerable through a hard-wired network connection, for example, through a clubhouse network outlet connected to the same network as the access control system. See the video, along with links to related information, at: http://www. bpforip.com/news/ip-based-readers-compromised.

Michael Gough got involved in examining the access control system because he is on the board of the association managing the pool property. As the only "tech person" on the board, he was the natural candidate to check into the problems they were having with the access control system. He was also personally curious as to why the system kept failing so often. As Gough commented to me, "The devices were developed before the Internet was used to manage them and so the design did not start by thinking of this connection.

The solution migrated to the Internet, though security improvements did not. It just worked, so why change?" That is a typical history for vulnerable products in this industry.

Gough also explained to me that, in his experience, the way security companies typically install such devices creates "default conditions" that are easily exploitable. That matches what my consulting and I colleagues have seen.

Why Don't Many Manufacturers Care?

I am often asked why the majority of manufacturers in this industry do not seem to care about network security and network architecture compatibility. I do not have a good answer for that, at least not a kind or charitable answer. Typical tradeshow responses range from arrogant dismissal, to unsubstantiated assurances, to blank stares. Every time I ask the "Why don't you care?" question at tradeshows, I am always told that the company does really care. If that is really the case, however, then *where is the evidence?* We should see it in the products and services and in their documentation.

For example, last week I talked to a company whose "About Us" web page claims "recognition" and "notable accomplishments" in networking and information technology. The company recommended for its product deployment a network architecture that was completely incompatible with their client's planned network architecture—a diagram of which I had sent well ahead of our phone call. So I listed for myself the possible reasons why such an off-base recommendation would be made by any company:

- The sales engineer does not understand typical enterprise networking.
- The product development team is software-savvy but not network-savvy.
- The sales and engineering people in the call did not look at the network diagram ahead of time.
- The product is poorly designed, and as a result the company is locked into a specific network architecture that it always recommends.
- The installed base is sufficiently small that the company has not encountered any enterprise-class networks in the field.
- The company has not surveyed the market landscape to determine what kinds of network environments its product would have to be deployed into.
- The company has not worked closely with any knowledgeable security technology design consultants.
- The vendor naïvely assumes that an extremely simple network architecture would naturally "just fit" into an enterprise network environment.

Not all of these reasons are likely to apply to every manufacturer; however, I was able to figure out that the majority of them did for this particular company. I have had similar experiences with other companies, small and large. How could there be such a mismatch between company capabilities (in this case the company is composed of high-powered professionals with good track records) and actual results? Could it be that they are just not talking to each other or to the right customers and service providers?

This made me realize that silos can exist in companies of every size. Maybe this is why the management personnel and the engineering personnel at many companies are not on the same page, with regards to network security and network architecture compatibility. Maybe this is why they do not have a good understanding of the customer deployment environments and don't seem to pool the information they do have regarding how their products fall short, including with regard to cyber security.

An IT Perspective

There is quite a difference in perspective between IT practitioners and physical security practitioners regarding what they expect from technology companies in relation to handling product security vulnerabilities. How would a security manager or technician, systems integrator, or security consultant report a security vulnerability found in a brand-name security system software or hardware product? While penning this work I performed a number of Google® searches, putting the names of big companies in the security industry in front of the phrase "security response center." The top responses for actual security response centers (not product or service pages) were for sites like Microsoft Security Response Center (MSRC), Symantec Security Response Center, Qwest Security Response Center, and the EMC Product Security Response Center—in other words, IT companies.

Here is a statement from the EMC Security Response Center website: "EMC follows industry best practices in managing and responding to security vulnerabilities in our products to minimize customers' risk of exposure." From the MSRC: "The mission of the Microsoft Security Response Center (MSRC) is to help our customers operate their systems and networks securely. A major part of this mission involves evaluating customers' reports of suspected vulnerabilities in Microsoft products and, when necessary, ensuring that patches and security bulletins that respond to bona fide reports are produced and disseminated." The point here is not to start a discussion about the security of EMC or Microsoft products, but to point out that more than a decade ago IT companies began to realize that their customers constitute a first line of discovery when it comes to product security vulnerabilities. Making it easy to report a problem would mean that more customers would do such reporting, providing valuable information on the impact of vulnerabilities, as well as a spectrum of technical details that would aid manufacturers in addressing product vulnerabilities. It's a win-win situation for customers and manufacturers.

Commitment to Customers' Interests

If you are a security industry manufacturer, or you represent a manufacturer or its products, how would you report a customer's concerns about product vulnerability? I'm not advocating that every industry company instantly set up a security response center. I am advocating that security industry companies start asking themselves this: "How are we going to live up to our 'best-in-class' assertions when it comes to minimizing customers' risk of exposure from product flaws or vulnerabilities."

Some Companies Do Care

Some companies definitely do care and are paying attention to product cyber security issues. *Brivo Systems* (www.brivo.com) has paid extensive attention to the secure engineering of their service offerings. In 2009 Brivo received both the SAS 70 type I and II certifications. These are based on the standards established by the American Institute of Certified Public Accountants, which assure customers that a service provider's controls and processes provide reasonable levels of service and data security.

Before its acquisition by Avigilon in 2013, the *RedCloud* physical access control product (now Avigilon's *Access Control Manager*; http://avigilon.com/products/access-control/) had a long-standing engagement with Veracode (www.veracode.com), a market-leading IT company that tests the security of independent software vendor applications. PlaSec has achieved the VerAfied rating (http://www.veracode.com/ratings), which means that none of the OWASP top 10 (https://www.owasp.org/index.php/Top_10_2013-Top_10) or CWE/SANS top 25 vulnerabilities (http://www.sans.org/top25-software-errors/) were found in the software.

"Customers are demanding independent proof that the software they are purchasing is secure," said Matt Moynahan, CEO of Veracode. "Given the rapidly growing threat posed by insecure software, PlaSec has established a leadership position in the market by demonstrating the security quality of their solution through Veracode's SecurityReview® service. Customers have a choice when making software purchasing decisions, and achieving the VerAfied security mark (http://www.veracode.com/ratings) provides a unique differentiator for PlaSec and shows their deep commitment to responding to an increasingly important customer concern."

Firetide (www.firetide.com) includes in their installation guide information on how to harden their network—an element that should be a part of any networked security systems installation instructions.

Someone recently commented to me about product and web service certifications, stating, "There is a lot more to product security than getting a certification." Of course there is. My response was, "Given other product features being equal, which product would you want your client to have—one that passed the certification tests or failed them?"

A few other companies have made similar good moves, and all companies who support their customers by making those moves should be applauded.

CONVERGENCE IN DESIGN: VIRTUAL CONSTRUCTION

Security technology convergence isn't just about putting security systems and devices on IP networks. It includes using advanced design technologies that the construction industry is strongly embracing, even while those technologies are still rapidly evolving.

> **Q: I am a long-time security consultant, and recently I was asked if I could provide a 3-D model of my security video system design for a prospective project. I haven't heard of this before, where can I find about it?**
>
> **A:** There is a lot of technology convergence going on in the field of building design and construction. This section provides some online references.

I was recently doing some homework for a presentation at the annual International Association of Professional Security Consultants (IAPSC) Annual Conference relating to this very subject. I was struck by how much convergence is going on within the building construction industry, and at a much faster pace than I was expecting. It's no wonder that the IAPSC wanted to have this topic covered at their conference.

Building Information Modeling

The National Building Information Model Standard Project Committee provides two official definitions of building information modeling (BIM):

- BIM is a digital representation of the physical and functional characteristics of a facility.
- A BIM is a shared knowledge resource for information about a facility, forming a reliable basis for decisions during its life cycle; defined as existing from earliest conception to demolition.

A BIM is not just a visual three-dimensional (3D) model; like the definition implies, it's an *information model* about a building.

Traditional Design and Construction

Before BIM, building design was based on architects' 3D scale models; two-dimensional (2D) drawings (such as those in Figures 2.1 and 2.2); and lists of doors, windows, equipment, and various materials needed to build the building

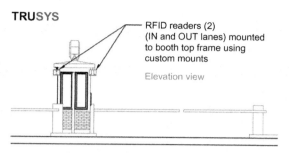

FIGURE 2.1
Elevation view of a parking control booth.

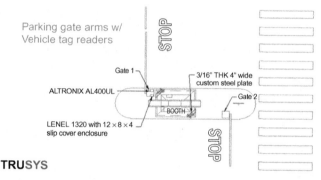

FIGURE 2.2
Plan view of a parking control booth.

as envisioned by the architects. Such plans constituted hundreds of pages of information that all had to be checked for conformance to the architect's ideas and for the compatibility of each piece of information with the other information in the plans. Errors occurred, and it was common for many of them not to be seen until construction was underway—with negative affects on cost and schedule since often work would have to be redone. As Kamran Moazami, Head of Discipline—Structures for WSP, one of the top global design firms, explains, "Construction cost overrun and waste is a normal industry practice even with the introduction of CAD and automated design since 1980." One of the key purposes of BIM is to make traditional building project waste and cost and schedule overruns things of the past.

Virtual Design and Construction

With BIM, the various design disciplines provide their information (or have it converted into) *information models* that conform to BIM standards, such as the *National BIM Standard—United States version 2* (www.nationalbimstandard. org). Drawings (both 2D and 3D), lists, schedules, and cost estimates are generated by a computer based on the BIM (Figure 2.3).

Referred to as virtual design and construction (VDC) a building is built first virtually, before physical construction begins. BIM software runs a clash detection algorithm on the building model to find problems in the design plans before the building is physically constructed. These then are corrected in the building's design and proven true in the virtual model.

Visualization

The 3D visualization capabilities of BIM software make it a powerful tool allowing builders and customers to visualize the intended result. Understanding of the intended final product is instantaneous upon seeing Figure 2.3. Contrast that with the time and effort required to build the same mental picture by studying the drawings shown in Figures 2.1 and 2.2, as well as the various equipment lists and product brochures relating to the design. Design decisions and customer approvals are reached in a fraction of the time required with a traditional building design approach.

Security Design and BIM

BIM models are built using smart objects that represent walls, doors, floors, equipment, plumbing, surface treatments—everything that goes into constructing a building. This can include security equipment.

Axis Communications has long provided network video design tools through its website and its architecture and engineering program. In 2013, Axis released

FIGURE 2.3
3D view of a parking control booth generated by BIM software.

a set of 3D CAD security camera interactive models for use with the Autodesk® Revit® CAD software, which is specifically built for BIM. Once incorporated into the overall design model, the camera models illustrate what the camera setup will look like in real life and which areas the video surveillance system will cover once installed.

When you drop a camera into the building model, camera information, such as focal range, resolution, and mounting options, as well as pixels per foot in the camera's field of view, becomes available. This significantly reduces the level of effort involved in design work and helps to detect obstructions that might not be obvious from reviewing 2D drawings. You can also get a 3D view of your CAD design, as seen through the lens of the Axis camera. Thus clients can easily review the 3D results of the video surveillance plan, which accurately reflect the fields of view that will be realized upon deployment.

As more and more companies provide product information as BIM models, more aspects of security design will be visualized in overall building models. Generic models of vehicles, people, and objects that are targets of detection and surveillance will be discoverable by the interactive models of intrusion detection sensors, long-range card readers, video analytics, and so on.

Valuable information on various aspects of the use of BIM in building design and construction can be found in the following online articles, videos, and presentations:

- *Got BIM?*
  www.slideshare.net/BeckyJDan/got-bim

- *5 tech trends transforming BIM/VDC*
  www.bdcnetwork.com/5-tech-trends-transforming-bimvdc

- *Axis Camera Families for Autodesk Revit (video)*
  www.axis.com/techsup/system_design_tools/camera_families/

- *ASSA ABLOY | OPENINGS STUDIO—for BIM and Beyond (video)*
  www.assaabloydss.com/en/local/dss/Openings-Studio/

- *World's tallest children's hospital pushes BIM to the extreme*
  http://bit.ly/BIM-to-the-extreme

ACKNOWLEDGMENTS

The author thanks TRUSYS, a global security and safety risk consultancy firm headquartered in Bellingham, Washington, with additional offices in Europe, the Middle East, and Southeast Asia, for providing the graphics for Figures 2.1–2.3.

CHAPTER 3

Physical Security and Information Technology Collaboration

The thirteen topics presented in this chapter present a variety of collaboration topics:

- Collaboration Between Physical Security and Information Technology
- How IT Can Help with Physical Security System Planning
- The Scope of Security Systems Integration
- Convergence Roles and Responsibilities
- Service-Level Agreements
- Security Video Requires Convergence Collaboration
- Data Security for Corporate Security Departments
- Financial Impact of Cyber Risk
- Protecting Information in Human Memory
- Network Protection for Security Systems
- Physical Security for Computing Systems
- Let IT Be Your Force Multiplier
- Security Patrols for Desktop Security

It is hoped that the range of topics covered is an indication that any topic you think may be worth collaborating on probably is.

COLLABORATION BETWEEN PHYSICAL SECURITY AND INFORMATION TECHNOLOGY

Collaboration between physical security and information technology (IT) functions is absolutely necessary to deploy current security systems. Earlier this year I learned that most, but not all, successful collaborations were initiated by a security manager who was, to some extent, IT savvy. Discussions that were not going well were initiated by someone who was not IT savvy. In-depth knowledge of IT, however, shouldn't be required simply to foster a productive dialog between physical security and IT functions.

Focusing on collaborations initiated by non-IT-savvy security practitioners, I found a key success factor common to all successful dialogs and missing in the rest. The successful collaborations all began with a very specific topic of discussion and technology objective. The topics and objectives were different but were all based on issues relating to existing or upcoming physical security projects. It seems that having a specific topic (as opposed to a broad general subject) on which to collaborate is more important than what that topic is. The stories of two security practitioners who have no background in IT make good examples.

Q: How did you initiate successful collaboration with your IT department?

A: It took almost three months for me to get the collaboration going. For some reason, IT couldn't identify the right individual to talk to me. I thought I was making myself clear when I said that we had some security projects coming up and needed to talk to IT about the convergence issues. Several IT people in succession had been assigned to talk to me. Each one said that they knew nothing about convergence and couldn't help.

We hit the point in budgetary planning where we absolutely needed to know whether or not the existing corporate network would support the communications of our planned security system upgrade. So to the very next IT person I said, "We need to know whether or not the existing corporate network can support our security system upgrade—we want to connect some of our systems over the wide area network." She asked in return, "Where are your systems located and what are the network requirements?" I responded by email, including maximum estimated bandwidth requirements based upon our video usage. The next thing you know I was in a meeting with three folks from IT, who brought maps, diagrams, and other information about the corporate network. We made great headway in that first meeting.

It was then that I realized had I been this specific in the first place, we would have been making progress from day one.

—Manager Security Systems & Technology, Major Insurance Company

A: Early in the project IT wouldn't assign IT resources to our project. We planned to install new systems for access control, alarm monitoring and video at 16 of our facilities, with local workstations at each facility, and a central command center where all the video and data would go via our network backbone. The IT folks kept saying that 20 workstations plus a few servers couldn't possibly require much work by IT. At the system integrator's insistence, we added a budget item for two IT full time personnel for a year. After the first two project meetings our IT representatives said that the project would require a full time IT project manager for a year and a half, plus assistance. They ended up hiring a new person just for our project.

Initially the way we had approached IT was simply to answer their questions about our project. We didn't know that we needed to go into detail about our video deployment. It wasn't discussed up front. Had we asked for one of the IT planners to attend our initial meetings with the RFP respondents, where we explained about our concept of operations for using the security technologies, we would have been off to a much better start with IT and avoided a number of project problems.

—Security Project Manager, Major Utility Company

HOW IT CAN HELP WITH PHYSICAL SECURITY SYSTEM PLANNING

One of the issues that security managers face when considering or planning the upgrade of a large physical access control system is accurately documenting the existing infrastructure and equipment. This is especially true for companies that have grown physically, whether by acquisition or by establishing new facilities. How do you pull all this information together?

This is a situation where the IT network personnel can help, because IT nearly always has up-to-date diagrams of the network infrastructure. If the physical security systems currently communicate over the network, then the network diagrams can be used as a basis for documenting the interconnections of the security systems. This information can be leveraged in a number of ways.

Q: What are some of the ways that IT has helped you with physical security system planning and assessment?

A: Our organization is moving from separate access control systems for our fifteen city-wide locations, to networked systems that we can manage centrally. This move has been long overdue and a recent security incident raised it to a high priority. Our documentation of systems was similarly separate, since each system was installed as a standalone system. IT had a Visio drawing of our city-wide network, and we were able to reuse that layout by removing the IT equipment and replacing it with icons for our own servers. That may sound like a small thing, but we were able to accomplish in a few hours what would have otherwise taken much longer, and literally overnight we had an accurate drawing that captured all of our access control and video servers, and which also documented the network we would use to connect the upgraded systems. It was easy to walk forward from there. What's more, the IT folks were already completely familiar with the drawing, and could readily participate in our planning discussions without advance study of the drawings.

—Security Manager, Public Service Organization

A: A recent power outage revealed some holes in our backup power scheme for devices and systems involved in intrusion detection and alarm reporting. Instead of addressing it on our own, as we have done in the past, we got IT involved rather than just consulting with the electricians. They provided us with an excellent CAD drawing plan of their own backup and emergency power scheme. We were able to add our own systems onto it as another layer, which really made it easy to see the whole picture. It turned out that they were considering an expansion of emergency power distribution for some of the IT systems, and we were able to roll many of our own requirements into their plan.

—Security Manager, Technical Services Company

THE SCOPE OF SECURITY SYSTEMS INTEGRATION

In previous years security integration meant bringing together access control, alarm monitoring, and closed-circuit TV systems at the security command console for surveillance and monitoring purposes, with some interaction between them so that alarms could, for example, trigger display of local video. Today this is practically a given, and is just one aspect of security systems integration.

The scope of security systems integration today incorporates human resources (HR) systems, identity management systems, and IT security systems and makes video available to company operations personnel for supervision, quality control, training, and metrics purposes. Today's integrations bring information into the realm of security, and often also bring along regulatory requirements relating to that information. Data from HR and identity management systems sources can have privacy implications, as can video information, depending on the circumstances.

Q: How has expanding the scope of your security systems integrations affected your collaborations with IT?

A: To make several improvements to our management of access control, we are automating our role-based provisioning of physical security access, using information from our HR system. Cancellations of security privileges will occur automatically when people are terminated, and privileges will be suspended during long vacation periods. Some of the access control readers will perform a time-clock function, and will automatically provide information to the HR payroll systems. Additionally, some personnel contact information will automatically be transferred to Security's emergency notification software, which is an off-site system designed to allow us to manage emergency incidents even if our corporate network is down or facilities become unoccupied.

This is where the privacy rules come into play, because some of the personnel information can't (according to company rules) go outside of our corporate network. Even within the network, access to certain information (such as home phone numbers) must be strictly controlled. Eventually, what personnel information our security staff can access—even within our own security systems—will be managed by our IT access control software. This way the existing policy-based IT security controls will be extended to relevant information in our security systems, and will be subject to the same audit procedures that are used to ensure corporate compliance for other systems. This takes the burden off of the Security department while still ensuring that our emergency response database is 100% up to date, which is critical. It closes a manual process security gap that we've had for a long time.

Along the way we're getting a better picture of how IT security functions, and our security systems are being brought into alignment with corporate compliance programs—just like the information systems of any other business unit.

—Security Manager, Global Manufacturing Company

A: In the past Security has been low on the priority list for IT response. Now that IT is getting an idea of the actual scope of our security operations and our risk-based orientation, a kind of "one-security-person-to-another camaraderie" has developed. We've been sharing information about how we apply risk management principles and prioritization to security measures, and it has helped make known the level of professionalism within our department. This has overflowed somewhat into IT services, and now we are given the level of service consideration that we deserve. We're also giving more consideration to the protection of IT infrastructure as we learn more about it, so it's a two-way street.

—Security Manager, Large Municipality

CONVERGENCE ROLES AND RESPONSIBILITIES

Several security managers and IT systems managers have recently written, in both questions and answers, about roles and responsibilities relating to security system technology being placed on their networks. Of course, the level of service that IT can provide depends on the size of the organization and its IT department.

Q: What roles and responsibilities has your IT department assumed with regard to physical security system technology placed onto the corporate network?

A: IT provides support to us for anything relating to networking. We specifically moved our security video servers into our corporate data centers, so that IT could manage the servers and data storage like they manage our other critical data systems. This provided us with RAID storage, data backup, redundant power, and so on. They basically guarantee that our security systems network communications will be up 24/7 year-round. We also use Virtual LANs to keep our video and other security traffic isolated from the rest of the LAN. Here is a list of the functions that IT provides for us with regard to our physical security systems:

Standards: IT provides standards for all computers and networked devices

Design: Network design and specification of network requirements, including bandwidth needs

Procurement: Purchasing of computer and network hardware

Software: Product evaluation, product configuration, and support

Project Mgmt: Project management for the network portions of our technology deployments

Testing: Leadership and participation in test planning and execution

Security: Computer and network security

Operations: Manage servers in our data centers

Storage: Manage storage for video and critical data

Transport: IP address management, video traffic management on the corporate backbone, network Quality of Service (QOS)

Remote Access: Remote access to our security systems via a security VPN

Our IT group works closely with our security systems integrators, whose technical personnel have a good rapport with the IT folks. Our troublesome technical problems went away once we got our IT group involved.

—Security Systems & Technology Manager, Global High-Tech Manufacturing Company

A: IT helps us with our network planning, and they make sure that we adhere to the published corporate IT standards. The IT standards include lifecycle planning, which was not an element of our technology planning until we learned about it from them. By following the standards, our computer and network equipment is "pre-approved" technology, which has shortened that aspect of our procurement cycle. IT has also participated in our systems integration with the HR system, and educated us about how to be compliant with our corporate data privacy policies.

—Security Manager, Global Manufacturing Company

SERVICE-LEVEL AGREEMENTS

In following up with several security managers and IT systems managers to discuss roles and responsibilities relating to security system technology on corporate networks, the subject of service-level agreements (SLAs) came up. IT departments have been using SLAs for over a decade (much longer if you consider contracts with telecom companies to be a form of SLA).

SLAs initially were used to define the responsibilities and requirements of external IT service providers. Several years ago, however, companies began using internal SLAs between the IT department and other departments to clearly define the levels of service needed and help IT direct its efforts and technology investments accordingly.

The security departments of a number of large corporations have SLAs with their IT departments to cover the services IT provides related to physical security systems IT maintains on the corporate network. Of course, many corporate security systems are maintained by systems integrators. Some security departments have received guidance and assistance from their IT departments in crafting SLAs for systems maintained by integrators.

An IT department's internal (rather than external) SLAs often provide the best examples for security systems SLAs because they are written for the same situation: The system end users in a department want to contract for an appropriate set of services. The answers here contain advice on using SLAs with an IT department. The same principles apply to establishing an SLA with a systems integrator.

Q: What advice do you have for security departments who want to implement an SLA with their IT department?

A: Make sure that IT understands which functions are most critical, and which are least critical. For example, if non-security personnel have access to the video system for supervisory or training or other business purposes, that's not as critical as the security workstations, which could be needed at any time for security incident response. Some managers and supervisors are on our incident response personnel list, because if there is an incident in one of their areas, we want them to have system access.

—Security Director, Water Utility

A: Although our IT department has SLAs with outside firms that incorporate some very technical language, we don't have lots of technical specifications in our SLAs for the security systems. It is very important to understand the entirety of each agreement (we have separate ones for network, server and workstation support services). Also the full scope of what you require from IT must be documented, including, for example, IT personnel getting vendor training. Fortunately the IT manager we worked with initially realized we were new to this, and we were able to "tweak" our agreements without pushback as we learned going forward.

—Security Tech Specialist, Food Manufacturing Company

SECURITY VIDEO REQUIRES CONVERGENCE COLLABORATION

One area of convergence has a significantly greater need for physical security and IT collaboration than any other area: security video system design and deployment. Specifying a megapixel camera where it is not appropriate can needlessly increase the bandwidth required by a particular camera. Even "where a camera points" can have an impact on the amount of network bandwidth required. The more continuous the motion in the camera's field of view, the lower the rate of data compression for the camera's video stream and the higher the bandwidth requirement. Including a busy street in the fields of view of multiple cameras—where only one or a few cameras would provide appropriate coverage of the scene—needlessly increases the size of the camera's data stream. These factors were simply not an issue with analog camera system design, in which each camera had its own cable connection back to the central monitoring point or recorder.

I recently talked with an IT specialist who used the term *video network engineering* to describe his work. He was completely unaware of the fact that physical aspects of a camera's field of view environment—and, consequently, the camera's placement—could impact its network requirements. Many other factors also impact a camera's network bandwidth requirement, such as the video frame rate (frames per second), which must be based on the role of the camera and what information the security (or quality of training) application needs to capture.

Most areas of technology convergence require more IT expertise than physical security expertise. Video system design and deployment is the significant exception. This is why IT systems integrators tackling video security projects need a video security specialist on board or as a partner (security consultants take note).

Many questions and problems center around one particular subject: *network bandwidth and the performance of networked video systems*. Several aspects of these responses are worth special attention. Here is a list of comments that typify responses; the most frequent comments are listed first:

- IT wants to know what our network requirements are for our security applications. We ask, "What kind of requirements, for example?" They reply with technical jargon that we don't understand.
- Initially, the video system was fine, but now the video display sometimes can't keep up when we use the point–tilt–zoom cameras. Once in a while, during investigations, we see the same thing with multiple operators on the video system. We haven't changed anything about the system.
- We want to move to an IP video system, but the IT department is saying that they want the security video system to have its own separate network and not be on the corporate network. That would make sharing video among managers and supervisors cost-prohibitive because we'd have to run the security network all through our facilities. Since recording uses a constant number of video streams, but viewing requires a variable number of fewer video streams, we think that we should use a separate network for recording and use the corporate network for viewing and video sharing. How do we determine the network requirements for each aspect of network use?

Many factors affect network performance for security system network traffic. To effectively plan and manage the use of any shared network for security systems (such as a corporate network), we must take those factors into account during the video system design and planning stage:

- Security systems traffic (nature and amount)
- Other traffic, such as data systems, voice over IP, Internet browsing, and so on (nature and amount)
- Wide-area network maximum and available bandwidth
- Number of individual video streams and maximum bandwidth requirement
- QOS requirements for security video
- QOS requirements for all other traffic
- Current and planned future use of the network

Be sure to cover these topics when collaborating about security video deployments.

DATA SECURITY FOR CORPORATE SECURITY DEPARTMENTS

IT departments in most medium and large organizations, and many small organizations, have three critically important policies that have a direct impact on security departments:

- *Computer and network use policy*—what is and is not acceptable use of the organization's computers and networks
- *Information systems security policy*—this typically requires antivirus and other computer and network security be applied to computers and networks
- *Data classification policy*—considers data is categorized based on criticality and sensitivity (such as confidential, private, and trade secret) to facilitate its protection

The names for these three policies vary: acceptable computer use policy or electronic media use policy; data security policy, information security policy, or network security policy; and data classification security policy or data classification standard, respectively.

Studying and understanding these policies is important for security directors and managers for many reasons. The policies apply to all computers and networks owned by the organization. Per these policies, "unapproved devices" are not allowed on the networks. Many policies forbid copying organizational nonpublic data (including video stills and clips) to USB memory sticks and other media. The policies also make the manager of a department (such as the security department) responsible for enforcing the policies in the department.

Data classification and information systems security policies usually establish the concept of "data owner," "data steward," or "business owner of data," meaning the person who is in charge of the area or department where the data are generated and/or used and who makes decisions about the use and handling of the data. The data owner is responsible for identifying all of the data that are generated and/or used and collaborating with a designated person in IT security to correctly classify the data and establish appropriate protective measures. For example, some security investigations material falls into the category of private employee information. Many policies mandate that such information (both hard copy and electronic) be handled in very specific ways. Below are some stories from security managers about their experiences in discovering these IT policies.

Q: Have any unexpected outcomes resulted from your physical security and IT department collaboration?

A: According to IT policy, the data generated by our security systems is classified as Sensitive Information and Critical. Critical information, by policy, is required to have high-assurance storage (such as raid hard drives) and specific data backup procedures. Here we had been trying to sell management on the need for upgrading our access control and video front end systems, and all along there was corporate policy mandating that we upgrade them!

—Security Manager, Global High-Tech Company

A: We have been sharing video clips with production area managers to support their safety and quality investigations. We recently learned that, according to company IT security policy, the CDs are supposed to be labeled with our company name and the words "Sensitive Information".
We are supposed to have a log of the CDs we issue. We are also supposed to have written procedures established for destroying the CDs after a certain amount of time. Had any of the information been misused (for example, posted on You Tube), I—the security manager—would have been culpable for non-compliance to company policy. Our DVRs store about 30 days of video, and old video is overwritten by new video, so although we didn't have a written policy covering data destruction, we did in effect have a general 30-day policy.

—Security Manager, Global Manufacturing Company

A: Our corporate data security policies have specific requirements for any network equipment rooms housing equipment through which Confidential or Private data is transmitted. This includes some means of physical access control and a log of persons physically accessing the rooms. Our IT department was actually in violation of their own policies, so we added card readers and door monitor switches to all of the equipment rooms. We created a report in the access control system that prints out a log of access granted and denied to all IT rooms, and we run that monthly for the IT group. When we were done with this project we had established an excellent rapport with the IT group, who now wants to put network cameras in a few critical equipment rooms, where multiple contractors have access to the rooms and on occasion IT equipment has been damaged with no clues as to how it was damaged.

—Manager, Security Systems, Engineering Services Firm

FINANCIAL IMPACT OF CYBER RISK

The Financial Management of Cyber Risk: An Implementation Framework for CFOs is a guide (originally released in 2008 under the title The Financial Impact of Cyber Risk: 50 Questions Every CFO Should Ask, see Figure 3.1) by the American National Standards Institute and the Internet Security Alliance that takes the topic of convergence to a whole new level.

THE FINANCIAL IMPACT OF CYBER RISK

50 QUESTIONS EVERY CFO SHOULD ASK

"Essential reading for CFOs"

— C. Warren Axelrod, Ph.D., CISM, CISSP
SVP, Bank of America
Author of Outsourcing Information Security

FIGURE 3.1
Original cover of The Financial Impact of Cyber Risk: 50 Questions Every CFO Should Ask, by the
American National Standards Institute and the Internet Security Alliance.

"We are experiencing a financial meltdown due to a fundamental misunderstanding and mismanagement of modern financial systems, which is generating a crisis of confidence in our core institutions. Today, all our critical infrastructures are reliant on cyber systems that are also misunderstood and mismanaged. These vulnerabilities place both our financial and physical security in jeopardy unless we update the method we use to control our cyber systems," said Larry Clinton, President of the Internet Security Alliance.

Developed by a cross-sector task force representing more than 30 private and public organizations, *The Financial Management of Cyber Risk* is the first known publication to approach the financial impact of cyber risks from the perspective of core business functions. It is available as a free download from the American National Standards Institute (http://webstore.ansi.org/cybersecurity.aspx).

The document provides guidance to chief financial officers and their colleagues responsible for legal issues, business operations and technology, risk management and transfer, and corporate communications. It is organized in a question-based format, which makes it applicable to virtually any industry and any set of business circumstances. The 76-page guide presents key questions for the following risk stakeholders:

- Chief legal counsel
- Chief compliance officer or chief privacy officer
- Business operations and technology teams (chief technology officer, chief security officer, chief information security officer and the disaster planning/business continuity planning groups)
- External communications and crisis management teams
- Risk manager for corporate insurance

Each question is accompanied by supporting information and guidance.

Appendix material provides a model of a simple method to look at current and expected probabilities of financial risk based on various levels of risk mitigation and two additional models (frequency and severity) for looking at risk caused by certain events. Also included is a list of applicable standards, frameworks, and guidance documents.

If your security responsibilities do not entail dealing with risk management at this level of your organization, this document provides an introduction to the types of cyber security risk issues that senior management is (or should be) dealing with.

As mentioned above, this guide is available online in PDF format at http://webstore.ansi.org/cybersecurity.aspx.

PROTECTING INFORMATION IN HUMAN MEMORY

Proprietary information exists in many forms, paper being one. Another huge category is electronic data, which includes data on hard drives, backup tapes, CDs and DVDs, and memory sticks, plus transmission data such as local and satellite radio waves, network data packets, and Internet data packets (including voice over IP telephone data).One form that is very challenging from an information protection standpoint is human memory and its related form, conversational data transmitted via sound vibrations in air waves.

Generations of spy movies have dealt with eavesdropping themes. The "eavesdrop" (an old form is also "eaves drip") is a spot on which water drips from eaves, which are the overhangs at the lower edge of a roof. Originally, an *eavesdropper* is a person who stood on the *eavesdrop* to listen in on conversations inside a house.

Some security measures that commonly are used to protect information in human memory form are employment contracts, nondisclosure agreements, and security awareness programs. Stepping outside of the security and HR and legal departments, however, one can find other organizational dynamics that can be highly effective in addressing some of the vulnerabilities that traditional measures don't fully address. The answer to the question below is one example.

Q: How have the current economic conditions impacted your security risks and your security program?

A: A voluntary or involuntary departure of any technical, sales or marketing staff is always of concern, given that the information they hold would be of very high value to our competitors. If a disgruntled employee is involved, the vulnerability can be serious, as the employee can feel "justified" in taking actions that harm the company. If a reduction in workforce is mandated, the information risks can skyrocket.

Our company goes well beyond "enforcement" of contractual terms, which is a weak security stance. Of course IT actively monitors the use of USB drives and CD drives to identify copying policy violations, since blanket automatic restriction of copying for some positions conflicts with job requirements. But that doesn't cover what the employees have in their heads.

We are fortunate in that our senior executives are well known and highly thought of in our industry, and we have a company culture that results from the situation that our senior executives genuinely care about our people. That helps us bring valuable personnel into the company.

A tough situation is one that we currently face, where we have recently hired some top talent away from other jobs, and we now have to let them go due to board mandates for workforce reduction. Personal admiration and trust is what brought these individuals to our company. It would be bad business ethics as well as bad public relations to simply turn them out onto the street, having cost them their previous employment positions. The senior executives who brought them in would lose their trust, something that has been built over the years. The trust and standing of our senior people in the local community and in our industry is part of our corporate value, and is an asset to be protected.

The challenge is to comply with the current board mandate in such a way that we not only protect that asset (trust and confidence), but retain the ability to rehire the employee when circumstances improve, which they will sooner or later. I'll explain how we address this security challenge strategically.

Our senior executives (marketing, engineering and sales) get on the telephone, and use their industry contacts to find new employment for our key people who will be let go. One security benefit is that by talking to the new employer, we can ensure that the new employer has terms in the employment contract that specifically cover not revealing information from our company. This is more proactive than most companies get, but that is a minor security measure. Helping the employees find a new job actually strengthens their trust and loyalty, and enhances our company reputation in spite of the negative circumstance. The strong personal and company loyalty engendered is the best security measure we have, as it is hard to consider any act against the people and company that are helping you.

Through this strategy to address the heightened risk, our security policy actually adds value to the company.

—Vice President, High-Tech Manufacturer

NETWORK PROTECTION FOR SECURITY SYSTEMS

Networked security systems have a variety of vulnerabilities, and even stand-alone systems are not vulnerability free. Security system networks can also have unique vulnerabilities that don't occur with business networks. The questions below were posed during a tech lab at ISC West around best practices for protecting IP-based security systems. You can download two white papers relating to this topic from www.BPforIP.com.

Below are several questions that I'm posing for you, the security practitioner, to answer.

Q: The corporate network is being attacked from an internal location. Your security systems are connected to it. How do you respond?

One security practitioner I know received such a notification. However, this would not happen for most companies given the typical project-based level of collaboration between physical/corporate security departments and the IT department. Security systems could be affected without the security department knowing what was going on.

What condition would warrant security being notified of a probable network attack? What response procedures would you follow? Most security technologists have not thought through these kinds of scenarios.

Q: A disgruntled employee has just taken out a lobby security camera with a taser. This also took out the network switch the camera was connected to. What should you do next to protect your security systems, in this kind of scenario?

Starting a few years ago, as part of security risk assessments, I and a few other security consultants began using Internet searches to help determine the likelihood of attacks that formerly would only be known about by people with special training. During one security assessment, a facilities engineer stated that he thinks every so often about the easy access to the transformers on the edge of the property; it would be easy to disable them using a particular technique (using a $3.00 item purchased at a hardware store). He said, "I don't think it's a serious concern because only trained engineers know about this vulnerability."

An Internet search instantly brought up a link to a website where the girlfriend of an engineer, who is a member of an activist group, described the attack in detail, including the $3.00 item needed. She wrote, "Use this approach to selectively take out power to specific facilities, rather than taking down an entire area, which might include hospitals or other healthcare facilities. You want to target businesses where loss of life is not the likely result."

Learning about the camera taser attack, I did an Internet search on that topic and found a YouTube video showing how to make a taser from a type of disposable camera available at most drugstores. What I thought was an attack that required the purchase of special equipment turned out not to be so expensive.

Rodney Thayer, a convergence engineer and founder of Smithee, Spelvin, Agnew, and Plinge (www.smithee.us), performed laboratory tests using a Graybar lighting arrestor connected between the camera and the network switch. Directly tasering the camera did not disable the network switch when the lighting arrestor was installed.

Most integrators use fiber modems to connect to outdoor cameras, specifically because of vulnerability to lightning. In addition, this keeps the network connection inside the building. However, I do know of two high-tech companies in the Bay Area that have installed network cameras outside their buildings, with a network connection going right to the camera. This is like opening an outside door to the server room, as far as the network switch is concerned.

Another important point about vulnerability to lightning is that the power behind a lightning strike is considerable. A lightning strike to a network camera connected by a copper cable may very well disable a series of network switches, not just the first connected switch. There is also the life-safety risk of impacting a technician working on any of the connected equipment.

Q: How would your IT department respond to a network attack that is coming from inside a facility, behind the corporate network's external

firewall? How would they detect, assess, and respond to such an attack? Do you have equivalent technical and procedural measures in place, either through security department capabilities or by a service agreement with IT?

The insider network attack scenario is worth exploring with IT because it can apply to security networks. How quickly can you tell when a network camera is disconnected from the network? Will it go undetected until the video loss is noticed, or will someone receive a video loss alarm? Are the cameras monitored the same way that critical IT equipment is monitored, so that the loss of the network connection is immediately reported? What about an IP card reader that's disconnected? Will that generate only an access control system alert to a security officer, or will network monitoring also provide notification to someone who can address the problem?

If you are still thinking of your security systems network as an *installed network*, then it is time to start thinking of and treating it as a *managed network*. You have, I hope, followed the IT department's standards and guidelines, so that the security systems network can be managed as well as the corporate business network can be managed.

PHYSICAL SECURITY FOR COMPUTING SYSTEMS

Physical security for computing systems is receiving increasing attention, in part because computers and network connections have moved out of environmentally secure locations (such as central computer rooms and tightly locked equipment closets) and into less environmentally secure offices, vehicles, and homes. Furthermore, the value of information available at any point of communication, storage, or presentation keeps increasing. The motivations to attack computing systems grow as the rewards for doing so increase. In relation to this, several practitioners have written asking questions like those below.

Q: IT is telling me that they want to collaborate about physical security for computer and network systems. They want to know what security event logs (access control?) we have that are relevant to IT. They want to know if our access management and intrusion alarm zones account for areas containing sensitive information. And they are asking to see our security strategies and policies. Where are these questions coming from? Is there some kind of reference or standard they are referring to?

A: Such questions are becoming more common. Most security managers responsible for facility security operations and technology think of convergence from the technology perspective, relating to placing physical security systems onto the network and having to comply with IT policy and standards. The questions coming from IT are about strategy and tactics. There are a number of references that could inspire such questions.

Developing a Plan for the Physical Protection of IT Systems

FIGURE 3.2
Cover of Michael Erbschloe's Physical Security for IT (Elsevier Digital Press, 2004).

An outstanding book that I have mentioned at least once before is *Physical Security for IT*, by Michael Erbschloe (See Figure 3.2). You can "Look Inside" that book on Amazon.com. Erbschloe provides specific advice on identifying physical security needs of network, computing, and communication systems. The book includes guidance on how to design and implement security plans to prevent the physical destruction of equipment or tampering with computers, network equipment, and telecommunications systems. More importantly, it includes an explanation of the processes for establishing a physical IT security function and contains illustrations of the major elements of a physical IT security plan, which outlines the way that an IT group would (and should) approach physical security. Readers will benefit by learning about sound strategy and planning approaches that also apply outside of the protection of IT systems.

Understanding Computing Systems Attacks and Defenses

To add a touch of reality to the kinds of attacks that are shown in movies and on TV, and to gain in-depth insight into computing systems attacks and defenses, download and read the 17-page paper "Physical Security Devices for Computer Subsystems: A Survey of Attacks and Defenses 2008," by Steve H. Weingart, available at: http://www.atsec.cn/downloads/pdf/phy_sec_dev.pdf. (See Figure 3.3).

This paper describes known physical attacks, ranging from simple attacks that require few skills or resources to complex attacks that require trained, technical people and considerable resources. High-tech protections are examined specifically, whereas low-tech approaches are only referenced because they are more commonly known. About 50% of the content concerns very sophisticated technical attacks that are of interest to chip designers and may relate to the packaging of electronic devices. All of the material is written in plain language and is easily readable, even for those without any background in IT. The paper definitely provides food for thought about both high-tech and low-tech methods.

Policy and Procedure Convergence

Many physical protective devices, especially low-tech devices, don't have electronic reporting mechanisms. Tamper-evident devices, for example, require visual inspection to observe evidence of tampering. This means that policy and procedure are critical to deploying such devices. This is a point of policy and procedural convergence. For example, what kind of audit practice should be implemented to ensure that breaches or attempted attacks are not missed? If an employee discovers a laptop has been physically tampered with, where could it have occurred? Was it at an airport or other location on a traveler security watch list? Who will take the report? Who will investigate? Should employee instructions regarding travel security be revised? The answers all relate to the value of the material being protected (both to the organization and to the attacker) and the impact of a breach or loss of data or a device. In other words, an information risk analysis is required to inform electronic and procedural security planning.

Most security measures selections are basic business sense. Once you know the asset to be protected, its value to the business, the impact of loss or exposure, its vulnerabilities and attractiveness, the level of general attacker interest, and the likelihood of a specific attack, then the degree and type of protections that various security measures can provide are one decision factor, along with the costs. The decision is a basic business decision.

FIGURE 3.3
Cover of "Physical Security Devices for Computer Subsystems: A Survey of Attacks and Defenses 2008" by Steve H. Weingart.

LET IT BE YOUR FORCE MULTIPLIER

Force multiplication, in military usage, refers to an attribute or a combination of attributes that makes a given force more effective than that same force would be without it. The question below came from a security manager who didn't realize that his company's IT department was offering to act as a significant force multiplier for the security department.

Q: What can I do about IT trying to take over my security technology projects? They want to insert all kinds of overhead and people into my projects, such as: project manager, requirements specialist, security and application architects, test specialist, network designer, and (believe it or not) a business analyst! We'll never get anything done! I want to get my project started, and they want to schedule meetings. It will take forever to get off the ground.

A: A smart response would be to book a conference room, order out for sandwiches and invite the group in for a two-hour lunch meeting. You've just been offered a high-power swat team that can save you time, effort and money—if you use them wisely.

No military field commander would complain too heavily about having to wait an hour for an air strike and artillery fire that will take out the enemy's high-power gun placements and let his troops cross the ground ahead swiftly and with zero loss of life. Instead of having each trooper duck and weave across the ground to try to make as poor a target as possible, the task becomes performing reconnaissance and perhaps drawing a little fire so as to identify the enemy's gun placements. This involves some strategic and tactical planning up front, with the end result of crossing the ground safely and much more quickly in the end, while significantly reducing the enemy's ability to counter the attack.

Security technology has changed significantly in the past decade. In many organizations, however, the approach to deploying security technology has remained the same.

SECURITY PATROLS FOR DESKTOP SECURITY

The question below relates to physical security supporting IT security.

Q: In our company our physical security system networks are independent of the business network. I suspect that there are benefits to convergence collaboration that we'd like to achieve, but I'm not sure where to start. Are there any "low hanging fruit" items to consider as first subjects for collaboration?

A: There are several but one of my favorites is Desktop Security, which may be a good starting point for collaboration.

IT departments often have their hands full with projects and operations and have a hard time monitoring compliance with corporate desktop security requirements. In reality, IT departments rarely have the personnel to inspect employee desk and workstation areas. Most companies have IT policies that assign the managers in each functional area to act as custodians for company computer equipment, but without some means of inspection and reporting it's difficult to effectively carry out such a scheme.

IT Policies

The nature of the desktop/work area inspections depends on the security measures specified in the related IT policies. Three common policies that contain instructions regarding computer and desktop security are the acceptable use policy (acceptable use of computers, networks, and information systems resources); the clean desktop policy (about not leaving any level of confidential or private information on the desktop or in unlocked drawers); and the information security policy. Sometimes the clean desktop elements are incorporated in the information security policy, but often they are extracted because the overall information security policy contains extensive other material that's not relevant to most personnel.

Typical requirements include items that can be inspected:

- Personnel must not leave their desktop computer or workstation unattended without logging out or locking their workstations.
- A screensaver with password protection must be used.
- Passwords must not be written down on sticky notes or slips of paper.
- Desks and filing cabinets must be locked at the end of the work day.
- Portable computing devices such as laptops and personal digital assistants must be locked away.
- CDs and DVDs, as well as USB drives (blank or empty or not), must be secured in a locked drawer.
- Desk drawers that contain company-restricted, confidential, or private information must be locked when the desk is unattended.

These policies often are available on the company intranet, but if you can't easily find them you should ask the IT Help Desk for a contact who can provide them.

Security Officer Patrols

IT has an electronic equivalent to security patrols: network monitoring and scanning software. Of course, this doesn't help with physical desktop inspections. That's where physical patrols by security officers can provide extra value to the company, adding a desktop inspection element to the security patrol plan.

It is usually feasible to divide the building areas into sections whose desktops can be inspected in 15 to 30 minutes, name or number the areas, and then put them on a list so that one or two areas can be inspected per afternoon or night shift patrol.

Desktop Inspections

Some companies have made printed sticky notes that contain a place for the date, the patrolling officer's name or initials, and the list of inspection items with a checkbox at the front of each item. If any violations are found, the inspecting officer marks the items and leaves one copy of the list on the desktop or another conspicuous place.

Before putting the inspections into effect, it is important to establish the actions that will be taken when violations are found and to notify employees in advance of inspections. Otherwise employees may feel blindsided, and this could have an unnecessary negative repercussion on security and IT.

Some typical actions are to log off computers and workstations that are usually left running and logged in and to confiscate sticky notes or papers containing passwords (placing them in a sealed envelope and securely storing them). Unlocked drawers may have a piece of yellow tape placed across them. Whether to confiscate company or personal laptops may depend on the specific work area. If confiscated, laptops must be securely stored and easily available for pickup so employees' work is not inhibited.

One company required repeat violators to attend a "Desktop Security Class," which was really a company-sponsored pizza lunch where a security officer briefed the offenders on the rationale behind the policies and the potential consequences of not rectifying computer and data vulnerabilities.

Exceptions

Collaborating with or briefing the area managers about the actions that will be taken for specific violations helps; any concerns can be raised and exceptions can be identified. For example, some laboratory laptops or workstations must be left running unattended when performing 24-hour actions.

RESULTS

The first few patrol inspections often find a number of violations. After word gets around, personnel begin to take the security requirements more seriously. Be sure to keep record of statistics on the type and number of violations found. It is a good return-on-investment point for security and IT both to be able to report 100% compliance with desktop security policy when achieved and to monitor it on an ongoing basis.

CHAPTER 4

Education Training

The phrase "convergence education and training" can be misleading in this sense: the vast majority of training and education topics that support convergence activities can't be found by searching the topic "convergence." They are named for the task that needs to be done or the aspect of technology, process, or procedure that the collaboration discussions are about.

RETURN ON INVESTMENT FOR CONVERGENCE EDUCATION AND TRAINING

One convergence issue for which there is a significant return on investment (ROI) is training and education. There is a broad requirement for education relating to convergence. The continuing incorporation of more and more information technology (IT) into security systems requires technical training for system technicians and installers, as well as sales people. Safely interconnecting security system networks and business networks requires knowledge of computer and network security. The physical protection of IT infrastructure (network cabling, data centers, telecommunications, and equipment rooms) requires training for IT and physical security personnel, at least enough to foster a dialog between the two groups. When security officer training includes some training on IT security, patrol officers become more productive as they make their rounds. Those organizations that have engaged in cross-training for their physical security and IT personnel, including their security managers, report both predicted and unpredicted benefits, providing an ROI that was greater than that expected by their security managers.

Q: How has cross-training and education on physical security and IT topics benefited your organization?

A: One long-standing problem for us has been the violations of desktop security policies. That includes non-computer issues, like leaving critical papers out or file cabinets unlocked. But it also includes computer desktop security violations like passwords written on post-it notes stuck to computer monitors, and laptops left running on the desk after hours where the user never logged out. The IT team doesn't have enough staff to walk around and check for these things, and that would be disruptive to do during business hours anyway. Our IT folks wouldn't feel comfortable with that kind of confrontation, so it has remained an unaddressed issue except when I would walk around myself and check offices and cubicles.

Then I realized we could train the security officers (who already patrol the buildings at night), to check for violations of desktop computer security policies. When violations are reported, we send daytime officers to the offenders to deliver a booklet on our desktop security policies, and provide a brief explanation of why these policies are important. Within 90 days we had a 54% reduction in desktop security violations.

We also equipped the officers with wireless "sniffers", so that they could detect rogue wireless access points not installed by our IT department. We could see them on our laptops when we opened them up in a conference room—we just didn't know where they were located. Our patrolling officers were able to find them.

Aside from the expected security benefits, we had an unexpected bonus in terms of sick day reduction. Prior to training the security officers on IT subjects, we had 20 to 30 sick days per month. In the first 90 days after we started our training program, we had zero sick days. A year later we still rarely see more than 10 sick days in a month. I don't know how else we could have accomplished that if we had tried.

—Chief Security Officer, Major Metropolitan City

A: This relates to a little "education" that I got, and additional training in our IT department. I was at a security conference and commented at lunch time that I was "off email" while attending the conference, because our IT department said that it was unsafe and too risky to allow me remote access. All of the other CSOs did have email and computer remote access. One of them was kind enough to tell me that it wasn't all that difficult to implement securely, and he explained the basics involved in plain English. Then he said, "When you go back, find out what your IT training budget is. This looks like a training issue to me." Sure enough, when I talked to the IT department, the training budget was next to nothing. Now instead of simply complaining as I had in the past, I knew exactly what kind of training to recommend. A few months later not only did I get remote access to email, but we instituted network security for our security systems network, and I also got secure access to our security system software as well.

—Security Manager, Construction Company

CERTIFICATIONS RELEVANT TO CONVERGENCE

While we can't provide an exhaustive list of all possible certifications here, we can provide feedback from security managers about the staff certifications they have found to be very helpful, especially with regard to convergence. While I was expecting to see IT certifications identified as most helpful regarding convergence, quite a number of managers stated that in their experience project management certification was most important. After giving that some thought I have to agree. Convergence has significantly increased the size, scope, and complexity of security projects, thereby increasing the need for project management skills. Correspondingly, I think that the Security Industry Association's development of the Certified Security Project Manager (CSPM) certification is an important industry advancement.

Q: What personnel certifications have you found helpful in dealing with convergence?

A: The most helpful certification to me is the project management certification. Several of my key security staff have the PMP certification: Project Management Professional from the Project Management Institute. As PMI identifies, the five key project management processes are "initiating, planning, executing, controlling, and closing." In my experience, most security departments have problems in one or more of these processes. In my 25 years in security it has been common to see security departments where projects can't get off the ground, planning is insufficient, execution is weak, and projects are poorly controlled or never seem to close. That's not to say that all of our projects run perfectly, but we do run a higher number of projects than most of my colleagues, and our projects run very well for the most part. We have also been able to help our systems integrators have better projects, and that benefits us both. If an integrator's project bogs down or gets into trouble, we can communicate accurately about the project deficiency and help get it on track. Most of the time we see that coming before the problem becomes too serious, and I attribute that to the knowledge and experience of our PMP certified staff. With regard to convergence, our company also has PMPs in IT. Our security project managers work well with the IT project managers, and that has been very beneficial for our large security infrastructure projects.

—Global Manager of Security Systems, High Tech Manufacturer

A: Many security techs in our key facilities now have a number of Microsoft and Cisco certifications. We got started on that education a few years ago. That came about basically because of recommendations from our IT group. It made it easier for our IT group to talk about their technology, and our technical staff established a better rapport with them. It also made our IT people more willing to share information because they knew their time would not be wasted.

—Security Manager, National Manufacturing Company

A: An interesting side-effect of our adding an MSCE and a CISSP certification to our security staff (the CISSP was our resident "computer guy") has been the discussions with IT and management around certification. Among our staff we have CPP and PSP certifications from ASIS, and NICET certifications for fire systems. They were not aware of these at all. When they learned about the scope of them, I could see their opinions of our staff changed a little. Recently two staff obtained college degrees (one in business management and one in criminal justice). I finally took to saying, "Don't let the uniforms fool you. They might all look alike in uniform, but we have quite a variety of education and skills among our security staff."

—Security Manager, Food Manufacturing Company

KNOWLEDGE GAP: CUSTOMERS AND SECURITY INTEGRATORS

Security practitioners at security conferences and meetings have begun voicing their frustrations about security integrators' lack of knowledge on the subject of convergence. The level of pent-up frustration among most practitioners was very high.

Q: Are you and your systems integrator on the same page with regard to convergence?

A: My own security techs know more about convergence than the techs my integrator employs. That makes me very uncomfortable about the recommendations I am getting.

—Security Manager, Manufacturer

A: My integrator has personnel who are very IT-savvy, but not security-savvy, and they don't seem to understand my application requirements.

—Director of Security & Safety, Insurance Company

A: My current integrator doesn't get along with my IT staff. My security staff gets along with them just fine. I can't tell where the problem lies, but guess what? I certainly can't get the IT staff replaced, so I only have one option, right?

—Security Manager, Food Manufacturing Company

A: My integrator is terrific on convergence. We're not on the same page, but he is slowly educating me and my security techs. Several times we've had end-of-the-day meetings where the integrator brings in dinner and we have a 3 hour education and brainstorming session. We included one of our IT guys in the last meeting, and that was really beneficial. It costs me a bit of overtime, but is well worth it.

—Director of Security & Safety, Real Estate Company

A: I'm dealing with a national integrator. Their sales and tech personnel are all over the map on convergence. Years ago we had no trouble doing a "look-ahead" into the future, and planning where we wanted to go with regard to the security technology in various regions. That is no longer the case, I think partly because of the rapid changes in security technology.

—Security Manager, Global High-Tech Company

LEARNING ABOUT INTERNET PROTOCOL-BASED SYSTEMS

According to statements and emails from physical security practitioners, getting educated on convergence-related technology topics can be a challenge. How much IT education do you need? How do you know what trainings are related to your current or planned security technology deployments?

Recently several individuals made the suggestion to address this challenge by taking advantage of vendor training—but not in the way I would have thought. I was impressed by the ingenuity involved and by how their approaches solved multiple problems.

Q: How do you address the challenge of education on the technology of IP-based systems?

A: We are a small systems integrator, and convergence education has been a significant challenge for both our own people and for our customers' personnel. For one project where we were competing against companies 10 times our size, the customer's IT department wasn't satisfied with the level of technical information available for any of the brands of systems being considered. IT wanted a clear understanding of what they would have to do to provide the first line of technical support. Our own technical personnel did not have all the answers they were looking for, and neither did their sales engineers. Additionally, the customer's IT personnel wanted to know what kind of a partner the vendor would be for them, and this was not something we could answer by experience.

Not having any other solution, we tried a radically new approach. We enrolled our own personnel and two of the customer's personnel in the vendor's installer training class—before the project was awarded. No purchase or decision had been made. During the training our customer's

IT technician asked questions no one else in the class was thinking about. The ensuing discussions were helpful for everyone in the class, especially for our own technicians. Because it was a group setting, none of the non-IT folks felt stupid because they weren't the only ones who didn't know about the issues. Fortunately the vendor's personnel didn't get defensive about the questions, but instead were willing to depart from the training agenda to delve deeper into some topics.

The customer asked the other integrators bidding the project to do the same thing for them, and neither the vendor involved or the integrator was unwilling to do so. We won this project and jumped way ahead in our convergence knowledge.

This also taught me that providing what the customer needs is paramount, and excelling at that can be a key competitive advantage no matter what the size of your company is.

—President and Owner, Security Systems Integrator

A: As a customer, one challenge I've had with regard to convergence is education for my staff who deal with the technology on a day-to-day basis. They are not new to security systems, and they always want to increase their knowledge beyond what is available in the vendors' customer training classes. In support of a recent RFP, we decided to send our personnel to the customer training classes for each vendor participating, prior to making an award. My personnel came back wanting to attend the installer's classes, which they learned about during one of their training trips.

That training was eye opening in many ways. Some vendors would not allow it. One product, which was a good product, would not have worked for us due to a few circumstances that are unique to our situation. The integrator proposing that system did not know about those details, and we would not have known to raise the issues. In the end we made a choice based on very solid knowledge not only of the systems, but also of the level of helpfulness that we could expect from the integrators and vendors. It's one of the smartest things we have ever done.

—Regional Security Director, Commercial Real Estate Management Company

MAXIMIZING YOUR PROGRESS IN THE NEW YEAR

Given today's risk trends and the current economic situations of most companies, the following question deserves more than a perfunctory answer.

Q: What kinds of New Year's resolutions are you seeing relating to security?

A: The typical New Year's resolutions that I have heard are these:

- Doing more on professional self-improvement
- Security program improvement, especially for better risk alignment
- Stopping the continued investment in outdated technology and finding a way to move to current-day technology despite financial constraints
- Getting my "convergence act" together

ASIS Annual Seminars Sessions

I am pleased to be able to write that some very valuable supporting material is available for these resolutions for somewhere between $99 and $199, depending on the status of your ASIS International membership and annual seminar attendance. What I'm referring to is the ASIS "deal of the century," as I call it—the purchase price for online access to, or DVDs of, audio and video recordings of nearly 200 educational sessions from the ASIS Annual Seminars. This still seems to be a little-known secret. Online-only access is $99 for members and DVDs plus online access is $149 for members. Since it is physically impossible to attend each of the 100+ sessions that I am interested in at the fall conference, I like to get the full set each year. Individual sessions can be purchased for $19 (online access only).

Starting in 2013 only the dual package (DVDs and online access) is available for $149. Annual seminars from 2005 through 2012 are available at: http://asisstore.confex.com/asisstore/. Annual seminars from 2013 are available at: https://asis.confex.com/asis/ansem2013/recordingpayment.cgi/.

I like to look over the list of sessions; prioritize based on what is applicable to client requirements, current trends, and my personal objectives; and set myself a program to review one or two sessions each week. For me this works out to be about $1 per session, and that's the highest value I can find in security education today.

ASIS Webinars

Another great value is the $99 annual subscription (member price) to ASIS webinars. ASIS members can purchase a webinar subscription allowing them to attend all ASIS-produced webinars through December 31 in the year the subscription is purchased except those with restricted access.

ASIS Member Council Participation

Another way to increase your personal knowledge and strengthen your security program is by actively participating in the ASIS Member Councils. In recent years there has been a significant increase in the level of work being done by the councils. They have developed and released each year several white papers on key security topics. I have met and worked with many fine people in the workshops and activities of the Physical Security Council and the IT Security Council.

The member councils are listed below. If a council seems like it may be a good match for your interests and responsibilities, go to the ASIS Member Council page (www.asisonline.org/councils) and reach out to one or more of the members listed on that page.

- Academic and Training Programs
- Banking and Financial Services
- Commercial Real Estate
- Crime and Loss Prevention
- Crisis Management and Business Continuity
- Cultural Properties
- Defense and Intelligence
- Economic Crime
- Fire and Life Safety
- Food Defense and Agriculture Security
- Gaming and Wagering Protection
- Global Terrorism and Political Instability
- Healthcare Security
- Hospitality, Entertainment, and Tourism Security
- Information Asset Protection and Pre-Employment Screening
- Information Technology Security
- Investigations
- Law Enforcement Liaison
- Leadership and Management Practices
- Military Liaison
- Petrochemical, Chemical, and Extractive Industry Security
- Pharmaceutical Security
- Physical Security
- Retail Loss Prevention
- School Safety And Security
- Security Architecture and Engineering
- Security Services
- Supply Chain and Transportation Security
- Utilities Security

Whatever your security New Year's resolutions are, you should be able to help yourself to some very useful support in one or more of the ways presented above.

CHAPTER 5

Security Planning

The four convergence topics in this chapter typically do not come to mind when most physical or information technology (IT) security practitioners think about convergence. Yet they are great topics because they apply to both physical security and IT security.

CONVERGENCE INITIATIVES: TIMING CAN BE CRITICAL

Putting security systems onto the corporate network should, of course, be done in accordance with corporate IT standards. Timing is an important consideration with regard to updating security communications infrastructure to make the move (migrate) from proprietary communications (e.g., coax and fiber for video, RS-485 for access control) to Ethernet network communications (wired and/or wireless).

According to projects I have seen, several potential timing factors apply to many organizations:

- When corporate networks are being partially or fully upgraded: Sometimes the security upgrade can be merged into that project and perhaps even be funded by it.
- When voice over internet protocol (VOIP) is being implemented: This almost always involves a network upgrade to provide a redundant and robust network that can run 24/7 for 365 days a year, which is what security needs.
- When facility construction is being planned: Work will usually be done on cabling infrastructure, and security's infrastructure upgrade could leverage this work and maybe even be rolled into the construction budget.
- When more cameras are needed: IP video can be started with a small set of network cameras and video management software that integrates both to existing digital video recorders and to network video recorders (NVRs) or NVR software.

- When more video storage is needed for higher video resolution or longer retention: An IP storage-attached network can be utilized to extend the storage of existing digital video recorders or NVRs.
- When planning the next year's budget: System life cycle planning should include migrating to network-based systems as soon as possible to take advantage of current and future technology capabilities (e.g., video analytics providing motion-based alarms not based on any motion but on detection of a specific object or behavior).

Some of the individual answers that I have received are printed below.

Q: What has driven the timing of your move to network-based security systems, and placing the systems onto the corporate network?

A: We needed to share video with manufacturing, quality, and supervisory personnel. That put our systems onto the corporate network. Manufacturing contributed funding to the project.

—Security Manager, Manufacturer

A: Our city implemented an upgrade to VOIP and network telephones, which involved a major network upgrade. Adding additional network capacity for security systems was just an incremental upgrade to the overall telephone network project.

—Security Manager, Major Metropolis

A: Our Global IT group recently issued an upgrade to their Network Policy and related standards. These documents contained several mandates. Any network based systems whose data is critical to the corporation be maintained in a data center environment. Any critical systems must be implemented in a high availability fashion (including redundant servers and power). Since security systems are critical to corporate operations, and security data is critical to the corporation, our server rooms must be upgraded to Data Center standards (including redundant power, plus HVAC and fire suppression standards), and our network hub rooms must be upgraded to the standards of the Network Equipment Rooms. In essence this was a mandate to upgrade our security systems and networks to be compatible with corporate networking, and so we put it into next year's budget.

—Security Manager, Global Fortune 500 Company

CONVERGENCE AND LAYERS OF SECURITY

I have been asked the question below a number of times, and one particularly important answer is provided.

Q: Does security technology convergence mean that I need to be thinking differently about how I use technology?

A: Although the quick answer is *yes*, thinking differently doesn't mean throwing away the perspectives about protective measures that have been effective in the past. Although security technology has changed significantly over the past decade, many traditional security perspectives haven't changed. One such perspective is *Layered Security*.

Over the years many readers have read at least some of the numerous articles and book chapters written on the topic of layered security. The reason I present the concept again here is that today's technology gains provide opportunities to significantly improve the security layers of our facilities, and so nearly all security technology plans deserve a good review from this perspective. Given today's economy, many discussions in trade journals and at security conferences revolved around upgrading or enhancing technology rather than replacing it. Most of these discussions are based on technology perspectives. Unless technology perspectives are coupled with a *security applications* perspective, there is low assurance of receiving the security benefit that could and should result from security technology planning. Layered security is one valuable application perspective.

Security Layers

Layered security is a design concept. It has also been called "concentric circles of protection" and "compartmentalization." This concept is part of the concepts included in crime prevention through environmental design (CPTED). The first illustration in *Facilities Physical Security Measures*, an ASIS guideline published in 2009 (free to members through the ASIS online bookstore), presents a simple layered security concept with three layers:

- Outer protective layer (e.g., natural or man-made barriers at a property line)
- Middle protective layer (e.g., exterior of a building)
- Inner protective layer (e.g., doors within a building)

As the standard states, starting on page 7, "One of the basic CPTED strategies is to design multiple or concentric layers of security measures so that highly protected assets are behind multiple barriers. These layers of security strategies or elements start from the outer perimeter and move inward to the area of the building with the greatest need for protection. Each layer is designed to delay an attacker as much as possible. This strategy is also known as *protection-in-depth* (Fay, 1993, p. 672). If properly planned, the delay should either discourage a penetration or assist in controlling it by providing time for an adequate response."

Understanding that the standard's layers of security illustration is an *example* of applying the design concept, and that you as a practitioner should apply the concept as appropriate for the facilities you are protecting, is important. The example is intentionally simple, whereas facilities are often more complex, having multiple buildings and multiple asset locations within each building.

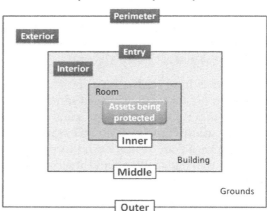

FIGURE 5.1

Illustration of layers of security, showing four layers of security: perimeter, exterior, entry, and interior.

Figure 5.1 expands on the picture presented in the ASIS standard, naming four layers of security (perimeter, exterior, entry, and interior) to facilitate thinking about how technology can be applied.

Security Functions by Layer

With respect to harmful actions against an asset, protective measures are intended to provide one or more of these basic functions:

- prevent (hazard condition or attempt by threat)
- deter (access or attack by an active threat)
- detect (presence of hazard or threat)
- delay (access or attack action)
- assess (situation)
- respond (by denying access, inhibiting attack actions, defending or protecting assets, minimizing consequences)
- recover (from effects of the attack)

One good way to approach technology design is to ask two questions for each security layer you have identified: what security functions should we implement? What technology will support those functions?

LEVELS OF SECURITY

This section follows up on the topic of the two previous sections, security layers, which describes an approach to relating security functions (prevent, deter, detect, delay, assess, respond, and recover) to facility zones or areas. Below we go one step further to consider the various types of technology that could be applied in each area.

Q: What is multimodal security?

A: Multimodal means *two modes* or *two methods*, which is a simple concept. If you send a package overseas it can travel by truck, train, and plane, or ship to its destination, and that is multimodal transportation. The term *"multimodal security,"* however, has actually been used in two ways. Sometimes it refers narrowly to a single device (a multimodal device); sometimes it means applying more than one security control or countermeasure at a single physical or logical point of security (multimodal security design).

Multimodal Devices

The most common such usage is with regard to two or more means of identity authentication for access control purposes. An example is the *plusID* device by Privaris (www.privaris.com), which is a personal biometric token (it looks like a key fob) that emulates up to four smart cards or proximity cards (such as the HID Corporate 1000 card). Using this device, biometric access can be added to practically any access controlled door without changing the door's card reader. It can be an affordable way to add biometric access to executive suites, data centers, network equipment rooms, research and development areas, and so on. (Space doesn't permit the description of the many other capabilities of *plusID* for both physical and logical security, which is why the Privaris website address is provided.)

The *plusID* product is one example of how multimodal security can be applied in a single device. A card reader with a keypad and biometric scan is another example of a multimodal device.

Multimodal Security Design

While multimodal devices dominate results for an Internet search of "multimodal security," a highly important use of the term refers to the security strategy of applying multiple security measures to an area or an access point. Multimodal security is an application of the *defense in depth* principle. This is also called *levels of security* or *levels of protection*. Although multiple levels of protection are sometimes referred to as "layers of security," it is more practical to save that term for the security being applied in physical or logical layers—like multiple rings or lines of protection—around a critical asset or along an access pathway, as described about.

Layers and Levels

Multiple security measures can provide highly effective protective and response capabilities, as well as redundancy, so that if one level or layer of security fails or is bypassed, others are still in effect. For example, a highly confidential formula for a high-performance lubricant (or a research sample of it) could be safeguarded by the following security measures, providing multiple layers and levels of protection:

- A two-person safe access rule
- A high-security electronic combination lock safe
- Both in-safe and external logs of contents added or removed
- Biometric access authentication
- One-time-use safe combinations
- Two-person rule enforced by an access control system
- A safe room access log
- Live video surveillance camera coverage
- Passive infrared motion detection
- Video-based motion detection
- Video recording
- Motion alert-based observation by a monitoring security officer
- Card reader access control for the room and the hall leading to the room
- Security officer patrols
- Strong background checks on the personnel who are given access to the area and to the safe itself, including the locksmith company personnel who install and service the safe
- Firm policies governing the use of the safe and its access
- Periodic audits of safe access records

Few areas or assets require this many layers and levels of protection, but all critical assets should have an appropriate number of protection layers and levels established and documented.

Security Functions

A simple security project to assess the adequacy of security measures is to (a) identify the critical assets and pathways to them, (b) document the layers and levels of protection being applied to each, and (c) determine whether improvements should be made. When considering improvements, the spectrum of security functions should be considered (prevent, deter, detect, delay, assess, respond, and recover) from the perspective of improving the number and strength of security functions in play for critical assets and areas.

WHY DO I NEED A TECHNOLOGY ROADMAP?

A September 2013 Internet search for "5-year technology roadmap" yielded over two million search results, including 5-year technology plans for countries, cities, and major universities. The IT departments of most large organizations have a technology roadmap for their IT infrastructure. Yet most security departments *don't* have a roadmap for their electronic security systems technology.

> **Q: Our company's new IT director asked me to provide him with a physical security technology roadmap. What is it and why do we need one?**
>
> **A:** A technology roadmap is a plan that shows the organization's needs relative to technology, and how technology will be applied to meet those needs. It is a primary means to build consensus for budgetary approvals and provides a framework for planning and coordinating technology deployments.

In small businesses, security technology planning is simpler. The owner/operator is involved enough in business operations to be aware of the obvious security risks, often after a security incident within the business or a neighboring business. The decisions are made by one or just a few people, and a security technology provider is engaged to install the desired technology.

In a larger organization responsibilities are divided across a number of executives and managers who have some specific function of the business as their primary focus. Actions that cut across or impact multiple business functions require coordination and planning and, most important, require that the key people be enlightened regarding the business reasons why proposed actions or expenditures are needed.

A technology roadmap is an effective tool for getting a sound plan, enlightening stakeholders, and gaining the organizational consensus and support needed for successfully planning and coordinating security technology deployment.

Furthermore, getting your act together by developing a security technology roadmap makes you and your security department worthy of the support and participation you will ask of others.

Developing the Business Case

Within most functional areas of the business, operational needs—including technology needs—can be easily identified. Outside of each functional area, there is usually little awareness of the function's technology needs. The needs must be clearly identified and documented so that they can be presented to the decision makers and planners, who are then enabled to approve initiatives and authorize the expenditures. Thus the phrase "business technology needs assessment" identifies over 49 million Internet search results.

To get high-level approval for significant security technology investments requires a *security technology needs assessment*, followed by a high-level plan of how specific technology will meet those needs, including what the costs will be and when the business can expect to start seeing results. That high-level plan is the *physical security technology roadmap*.

Security Systems are IT Systems

Electronic security systems are IT systems because they are a computerized network of intelligent devices and sensors. This is one reason why it is completely appropriate for corporate security departments to follow the customary IT approach: (a) assess the technology needs of the business and (b) develop a sound technology roadmap.

There is an abundance of material on the Internet that applies to small, medium, and large businesses, including templates and "how-to" information for technology needs assessments. Most of the technology needs assessment material targets computer and network technology, but it can also be successfully applied to physical security technology, remembering that *cost-effective security risk reduction* is the overarching business objective and is the only justification for security technology deployment.

Lunch Roadmap Briefing

If your IT department has a technology roadmap, you will probably find that it is captured in two documents: a detailed roadmap document and a slide presentation for management. Get an introduction to the person who developed the roadmap or was an active part of the roadmap development team, and arrange a lunch meeting so you can be briefed on the roadmap development process; have the documents reviewed with you and your technology specialist.

Here are some of the many reasons to arrange such a briefing:

- Find out how technology roadmap development has been successfully done within your organization.
- Understand the plans for network infrastructure growth to know what network infrastructure will be available for security systems.
- Discover what technology support resources are in place or planned that could help with security systems deployment.
- Become aware of about the process IT uses to develop its technology standards and approved products list.
- Learn more about the policies and procedures that IT applies to technology deployment so that security can apply the appropriate ones to achieve smoother deployments.

Roadmap Dividends

However you approach it, the process of developing a sound physical security technology roadmap will open doors and establish alliances that have both immediate and long-term dividends.

CHAPTER 6

Convergent Impacts on Security Design

This chapter's topics deal with technical design factors that are easy to understand yet are often a source of trouble. You may already have collided with a few of them yourself.

POWER OVER ETHERNET

With regard to network video, one particular technology warrants special attention: *Power over Ethernet* (PoE). Many companies are updating their network infrastructures with PoE capability for *IP telephones*, providing an infrastructure that is compatible with *IP cameras*, also known as *network cameras*, that are PoE-enabled. This is good news for security in such companies, but to achieve the maximum benefit (and to avoid unnecessary expenditures), security must collaborate with the IT department about any immediate or future network camera deployment early in the network upgrade planning. This column first addresses PoE with regard to video systems planning and deployment and ends with an important note about deploying other types of PoE-enabled security devices.

Wikipedia (the free online encyclopedia) provides a good article on PoE, which begins with the following definition:

> Power over Ethernet or PoE describes any of several standardized or ad-hoc systems which pass electrical power along with data on Ethernet cabling. This allows a single cable to provide both data connection and electrical power to devices such as wireless access points or IP cameras. Unlike standards such as Universal Serial Bus [USB] which also power devices over the data cables, PoE allows long cable lengths. Power may be carried on the same conductors as the data, or it may be carried on dedicated conductors in the same cable.

Previously the PoE specification (802.3 af) limited PoE-supplied power to 15 W at 48 V. An update to the specification (802.3 at) doubled the power to 25.5 W. This supports devices such as Pan-Tilt-Zoom (PTZ) cameras, which require more than 15 W of power. For more information, including references to possible prestandard PoE devices that may exist in networks, see the Wikipedia article (http://en.wikipedia.org/wiki/Power_over_Ethernet).

IP Telephones

IP telephones combine voice over IP and PoE technologies and use a single PoE-enabled network connection for both power and data, which can be used for voice data alone or for voice and video data (video phones). The cost savings and manageability of IP telephones are major reasons why many companies are upgrading their corporate network infrastructure to support them.

Early collaboration with IT is important if your company is upgrading to IP telephones and you'd like to take advantage of the network for IP video. Such newly upgraded network infrastructure will be compatible with PoE-enabled network cameras, but that doesn't mean that the network's PoE *power capacity* will be sufficient to support an array of network cameras. Arranging that capacity in advance is generally much less expensive and troublesome than arranging it after IT's network upgrade is completed. In addition to IP telephones, there may be other PoE devices on the network, such as wireless access points.

Advanced Planning with IT is Critical

For example, the Catalyst 6500 network switch from Cisco, used to provide PoE-enabled network connections for IP telephones, can be configured to provide either 1300 or 2500 W in a power-redundant mode, which uses two power supplies; if one fails, the other still provides full power. (There are other power options, but this example references only two of them for the sake of illustration.) An IP phone can require anywhere between 4 and 10 W of power per phone, depending on the make and model. An IP camera can require anywhere between 7 and 20 W per camera, depending on make and model. If IT plans to use the switch to support 120 phones at 10 W each plus some other PoE-powered equipment and configures the switch for 1300 W, there won't be any power left over for network cameras. If the switch is configured for 2500 W to account for camera power, however, about 50 network cameras, each requiring 20 W, could be supported.

Having to support 50 cameras on a single network switch is not common simply because the portion of the facility or campus that is being supported by the switch is not likely to have that many cameras. However, the example does illustrate the point that in one power configuration, a switch's power capacity can be used up by telephones and won't be able to support cameras, yet in another configuration it can provide for cameras more power than will be needed. The price difference between the example configurations would be in the neighborhood of $500 at the time of original planning—and the procurement and deployment costs would be part of the existing IT budget. However, the cost to upgrade afterward (i.e., after the IT project is complete) would be many times that, with security having to foot the bill for the after-the-fact upgrade to power the cameras.

As an aid to planning, Cisco Systems provides an online tool, the Cisco® Power Calculator, which enables calculation of the power supply requirements for specific PoE configurations. This tool takes into account the internal power requirements of a Cisco network switch based on the options installed in the switch. Access the power calculator tool at http://tools.cisco.com/cpc/launch.jsp/ (requires registration to use).

There are many more details to take into consideration, such as network bandwidth and quality of service configuration for IP camera network traffic. These and other engineering considerations mean that when IT infrastructure upgrades are planned, security can benefit greatly by collaborating in the planning so that their requirements are a small incremental addition to what IT has already planned.

Below are two answers to a question on this topic that shed light on some current and future aspects of placing PoE-enabled security devices onto a corporate network.

Q: What kinds of technical issues have you encountered in placing security systems onto the corporate network?

A: Be certain when checking the power delivery capabilities of a network switch to ensure it is 802.3 af compatible. A pre-standards version to PoE is Cisco's *inline power*, which only delivers a maximum of about 9 W to an *inline power* compatible device. This may not be enough for a video camera. There are still some switches in service that use *inline power* only such as the Catalyst 3524XL 24PWR.

It is also important to test that devices negotiate power with the switch correctly. For example, I've seen a timecard reader (time and attendance) fail to draw power from a switch even though the vendor claimed it was 802.3 af compatible. I've seen the same thing when mixing networking vendor equipment, for example, Avaya IP phones on Cisco switches or Cisco wireless access points on Foundry switches. There may be extra configuration work required to get the devices to work together.

—Network Specialist, High Tech Company

A: In addition to the technical aspects of PoE, other aspects are emerging that will require attention, especially as card readers and alarm devices move onto the network. For example, there are life safety code compliance considerations, and the relationship of the interface between fire alarm system and the access control system.

—Shayne Bates – leading security strategist, advisor and advocate

PHYSICAL SECURITY INFORMATION MANAGEMENT AND DATA: WHAT'S THE DIFFERENCE?

A friend of mine from the IT world recently expressed his bafflement that physical security practitioners would tolerate the possibility of loss of video due to DVR hard drive failure, especially since redundant array of independent disks data protection (http://en.wikipedia.org/wiki/RAID) is more than a decade old.

"They call it a 'DATA center,'" he said, "because safeguarding corporate data, and ensuring its availability, is mission critical. Video data is critical data, so why don't security managers simply follow their company's standard practices for critical data?" That's a good question.

One reason is that previous security video recording products have not followed IT standards or practices. DVRs were developed as replacements for VCRs, and were not designed or intended to fulfill data center requirements. That's just the history of it—a history that is not generally known by IT specialists.

What was interesting in the conversation is that my friend had uttered the word *data* as if simply speaking that "magical word" was somehow the answer to the situation. That's no surprise; in the IT world data infrastructure is a respected discipline. The term *data infrastructure* refers to shared networked storage systems that safeguard the data, ensure that it is available as needed, and facilitate management of the shared storage resources. At the end of the day, *data* remains a core critical asset. And, as the organization's information needs grow, a sound data infrastructure supports that growth without needing to rip and replace storage systems. (An excellent four-page white paper by the Uptime Institute defines what constitutes a "reliable data center" http://www.go-rbcs.com/reliable-data-center. You can see where your own security systems rate within the clearly defined scale provided.)

This discussion reminded me of a question I had received by email:

Q: What will it take to get the physical security folks to "see the light" about DATA?

My initial response was another question, "Which security folks are we talking about?" Other questions follow that one: "Which data should they be concerned about?" and "What's the difference between PSIM (physical security information management) and data management?"

Data is an abstract term, initially used by people who design and maintain the systems that hold or transmit information. They don't deal with the information itself. From their perspective, data are bits and bytes needing storage capacity and network bandwidth. It's an abstract term at the systems level of thinking. Data management is what a good storage system allows you to do. Information management is what a good information system allows you to do, and that's where PSIM comes in.

At the security operations level, it's not *data*—its *evidence, intel,* or *activity*. It's *information*. Video systems capture accidents, incidents, people, vehicles, and objects. Recorded video must answer the question, "What happened?" If it can't answer that question, it is of no value. Ask the security practitioner whose video system did not capture a critical incident or whose recorded video doesn't clearly reveal what has occurred. You can't use or manage information that you don't have.

Providing a robust (i.e., fault-tolerant) high-performance data infrastructure is how you guarantee that critical video data is available when you need it. In the future perhaps all security data will safely reside in an IT data center environment. Until then, there is every reason to establish *data center-quality* data infrastructure not just for video data, but for access control and other security systems data. The more advanced PSIM applications become, the more important the data infrastructure is.

Another key point is that the design of IT data infrastructure not only provides the reliability and performance needed for critical data applications, it provides it *affordably*. In today's economic environment, that's an important issue. As security risks escalate, the importance of security system data increases. Yet most video systems today record at lower frame rates and resolutions than the cameras provide. In addition, general surveys of practitioners tend to indicate that video retention rates are about half of what security needs would dictate. That's most often the case because the high cost of non-IT video storage forced compromises in the design of video storage for budget compliance.

That has left many security practitioners in the situation where they had no choice but to accept recording video at one-half or one-quarter of the quality (resolution and frame rate) that the camera puts out. Many new DVRs are still limited in that regard.

In the past it has been hard to think of recorded video as *critical data* because the video coverage was often incomplete and the recorded quality less than desirable. It's not critical data if it doesn't contain the necessary information.

With the affordability and capability of today's video technology, there is no reason to settle for less than what the job of security requires.

IMPACT: THE PACE OF TECHNOLOGY DEVELOPMENT

Each year security practitioners ask how to deal with the increasing pace of technology development. To try to get a sense of the impact, the question below is the one I have been asking in return. The answers cover a spectrum that is too broad to address in a single column, so I'll start with those that invalidated some of my previously successful practices.

Q: How has the pace of security technology development affected you?

A: When it comes to evaluating technology, it used to be that I could check with a few reference sites and see what kind of experience they had, and get a good idea of how it would work for my client in actual operations. These were usually simple and straightforward conversations. In the past there was generally uniformity in the answers for a particular brand or product. Either all the experiences were good to great, or they were mildly to significantly unsatisfactory. Now I'm finding that's not the case anymore. The same system can have good performance for some, and not for others. More recently I have tried to find out why. After ruling out dissatisfaction due to overly high expectations, and known compromises for the sake of cost, there were still differences in product and system performance. Sometimes the selected technology was (in my opinion) not the right recommendation for that particular end user's needs. Sometimes the technology was simply not configured properly, which would be a shortcoming of the integrator. Sometimes the end users didn't know how to use the product in the way they needed to, even though the functionality was there. I have also seen systems that when I observed them, looked great to me, yet the end users said they preferred another system they saw at a similar facility (one that I don't think is as good as what they have). My main conclusion is that it now requires a lot more homework to "get it right" than it used to, especially with the rapid pace of technology change.

—Veteran Security Technology Consultant

A: We now always pilot test any strategic technology, no matter what we see elsewhere. It has always turned out to be worth the cost. Many times we have saved some big missteps that would have occurred with our global deployments. They would have compromised our security performance, and lowered the credibility of our security team.

—Global Security Manager, IT Software and Services Company

In a very frank discussion of the capabilities of network video cameras, Fredrik Nilsson of Axis Communications explains (in his book *Intelligent Network Video*), "To properly compare the low-light performance of two different cameras, it is necessary to look beyond the lux and IRE numbers. Putting two cameras side by side and comparing the outcome is recommended."

When you are closely examining specific product performance, the target environment can have a lot to do with the performance outcome, especially with cameras. Unless you can find an environment that is identical to yours and is using the technology in exactly the same way, a pilot test is the surest way to guarantee that you get what you want. It is a small cost to guarantee that "what you see is what you get," which is important when it comes to something as critical as security.

TECHNOLOGY BLINDERS

Many security practitioners ask whether there are any special technologies that they should be paying attention to given the current economic climate and its impacts on corporate budgets, including security budgets. There are technologies, for instance, that can extend the useful life of existing systems and cabling infrastructure. Some technologies are force multipliers, allowing fewer people to do more. Some let you bridge from analog systems to IP-based systems (networked systems) on a very affordable step-by-step basis.

Technology Blinders

Before presenting answers of this variety, however, it is important to step back and take a look at the bigger picture.

When engaging in security analysis and when discussing security with people outside of security and IT, it's important that enthusiasm for new high-tech security systems and products doesn't create blinders that keep low-tech solutions out of view. This is a risk for those in both IT and security who are immersed in technology on a daily basis.

Emil Marone, Chief Technology Officer of Henry Bros. Electronics, a large integrator headquartered in Fair Lawn, NH, relates one situation where a client called him in to discuss a problem they were having with night intruders on their property. The intruders would dress in black and could not easily be seen against the black asphalt and dark grounds of the perimeter under the existing lighting. They were considering a new CCTV system that could "see in the dark" and were also considering a complete renovation of their outdoor lighting. Both measures would be expensive and disruptive, but these improvements seemed to be needed to solve their problem.

"Once I had an understanding of the situation," said Marone, "I advised against making either change. Cameras that can see in the dark won't help the security officers on foot patrol, and there was a better solution available." Marone suggested that they simply paint the grounds white on both sides of the perimeter fencing. Intruders dressed in black would be clearly visible. Even in white clothes they would still create obvious shadows under the existing lighting. It was a very inexpensive solution and was implemented immediately with great success. This approach enabled both the foot patrols and the personnel monitoring the CCTV images to see what they needed to see.

A broader aspect of technology blinders is the focus on technology solutions while neglecting people and process solutions—which are often more quickly and easily implemented for little or no budgetary expense. With risks increasing because of the current economic situation, security programs must be updated using whatever resources can be put to use.

Impacts of Today's Economics

Many companies are making reductions in head count in response to the need to cut expenses. This creates additional risks, including for property and information loss. Are exit and perimeter door cameras still functioning as intended, or has cleaning crew activity accidentally changed any fields of view? A quick review of camera focus, fields of view, and scene lighting can identify issues that are easily corrected. Are property passes given the full scrutiny that they should receive and checked against items being removed? What is the policy for the loss of company-owned laptop computers? Do exit interviews remind the departing employee of confidentiality requirements (with signature required)?

Can and does IT alert the security department of an unusually high level of material copying activity? Is remote computer system access and after-hours physical access suspended upon notice of termination, rather than after the employee has left? Are other appropriate security measures put in place?

IT departments are typically not set up to interview or brief employees, but security and HR departments are. When the data access of departing employees is restricted, departing employees can ask colleagues to copy information for them. The favor is likely to be granted if the excuse for doing so seems reasonable—unless employees are briefed about this potential situation.

An updated protection strategy is required for both information system and physical security during downsizing. A survey conducted in 2009 by the Ponemon Institute and sponsored by Symantec Corporation reveals that more than half of departing employees steal corporate data. This study's 24-page report, titled "Data Loss Risks During Downsizing," is available at: http://www.symantec.com/connect/blogs/data-loss-risks-during-downsizing-new-report. Security and HR practitioners, as well as management, need to be aware of this report's contents and follow up to address the relevant risks.

ADDRESSING RISKS IN REAL TIME

Q: What convergence technologies or applications can help address risks in real time?

Due to the continuing rapid advancement of digital technologies, this question is asked by many attendees of annual security trade shows and conferences. One demonstration of real-time risk mitigation appealed to me above others, because the use of the two technologies enables coordinated *detection* and *response* for both cyber and physical security threats across the two domains.

Real-Time Correlation of the Virtual World and the Physical World

ArcSight (www.arcsight.com) is a visionary company whose *Enterprise Security Manager* is a leading product in the IT domain. Classified as a *security information and event management* tool, it contains an optional *Threat Response Manager* (TRM) module that not only can detect new risk conditions in real time but also can take immediate remedial action in as well (all based on rules made specifically for your business and its facilities). For example, if an access-controlled space containing critical data or materials is propped open, TRM can lock down the next layer of doors, extending the access restrictions outward to the next access control layer, keeping the data or materials safe and keeping regulatory compliance intact. It can also notify security of the change—enabling officers to correctly deal with the temporary changes in access privileges. Furthermore, it can also notify security of individuals who were already inside the newly extended protection zone at the time of the response, providing accurate situational awareness in seconds. Executing such a response through security officer procedures would be extremely difficult, and executing it in the near-immediate time frame of the systems would be impossible.

To implement this kind of capability requires that ArcSight's *Enterprise Security Manager* is integrated with a physical access control system such as Avigilon's *Access Control Manager 5.0*, which can exchange data with *Enterprise Security Manager* and accept response actions generated by its TRM module.

It's a Two-Way Street

Responses to events in either domain can trigger an appropriate response from both domains, since the two worlds now have a rules-based correlation. For example, if an *authorized* physical access to a network equipment room occurred, followed by an *unauthorized* logical change (such as a configuration change prohibited by IT policy) to any of the network equipment in that room, *Enterprise Security Manager* can lock down the network ports in that room, preventing someone from using a laptop computer to log on to any data systems or networks from inside the room. Furthermore, *Enterprise Security Manager* can generate the same kind of response in the *Access Control Manager* system (an alarm event on the alarm monitoring screen, triggering the display-related video on the overhead screens) that would automatically occur for a physical access violation or unauthorized access attempt at the network equipment room door. Thus security officers would know that an IT security incident was in progress and could more properly interpret physical events in the vicinity. These examples just scratch the surface of what can be done.

Ease of Integration

ArcSight has developed a standard for promoting interoperability between various event- or log-generating devices, called the common event format (CEF). It can be readily adopted by vendors of both security and nonsecurity devices. After an ASIS conference, I contacted ArcSight and asked them for information on CEF. In addition to their CEF White Paper, I also received the Avigilon *Certified CEF Configuration Guide*, which contains three pages of instructions for activating the ArcSight CEF connector, followed by an eight-page listing of how the data fields map from Access Control Manager events to the ArcSight CEF format. The integration is easy and can be set up in minutes. The two devices (ArcSight's and Access Control Manager's) communicate via the network.

The remainder of the work is setting up *Enterprise Security Manager* and its *TRM* to recognize threats and vulnerabilities (i.e., risk conditions) and define appropriate responses. *Planning what to do* (i.e., the operational security responses) takes the most time. After an introduction to the TRM, setting up the rules and defining the responses is straightforward.

This is technology that puts the security practitioner in the driver's seat with regard to a converged approach to real-time risk detection and response.

WHO SPECIFIED THIS?

This is a common question that I have heard from integrators, end-user customers, and consultants (including me) who have been called in to troubleshoot a problem situation with a particular system or piece of technology.

Q: Who specified this?

A: No one did.

System Design versus Product Selection

The question and answer above identify the root cause of a great many problems with facility physical security system deployments. The system or product wasn't actually *specified*. It was selected, recommended, bid, quoted, copied, or searched for on the Internet. Products are selected at trade shows, recommended by systems integrators, bid or quoted in response to a request from a customer. They are copied from what was seen at other facilities. Sometimes they are selected simply from information found on vendor websites. When that happens outside the context of a sound security design effort, trouble follows.

In his book *Security Design Consulting: The Business of Security System Design*, Brian Gouin, a physical security professional and certified security consultant (CSC), says:

> With the growing complexity of technology in the security industry and the relatively poor quality system design work within that industry, there is a growing need for design professionals specifically trained and working in the security field.

Only after a security designer has obtained a thorough understanding of a facility's security needs can a specific product be matched to those needs. Even then, it has to be done according to the concept of security operations in which specific product and system functions will be utilized.

Role of Security System Design

The International Association of Professional Security Consultants (IAPSC) knows that I would periodically send a security manager client to their 2-day program titled, "The Successful Security Consultant," held as a seminar program before the ASIS International annual seminars.

Other consultants occasionally would question my sanity in doing so, asserting that I could be "doing myself out of a job" by having my clients learn how to perform the work of a security consultant. Quite the contrary: This kind of comment shows a real lack of insight into the life of a security operations manager.

No security operations managers have the time to actually perform the work of a security design consultant, but they do have a need to understand it. In fact, some of the most effective security managers I have known are those who were security consultants before being hired as a security manager. With regard to my own consulting projects, I definitely want to have a client who understands and appreciates the work that I do and who also knows what is expected and needed from them when they embark on a significant security technology deployment.

While explaining my preference for educated clients to one consultant a few years ago, I was surprised to see the horrified look on his face as he said, "You had better watch out. Knowledge is power." Of course it is! I *want* empowered clients who know how to represent their security agendas to management and to budget decision makers, who can tell the difference between a good and a bad Request For Proposal (RFP) response, and who know how to insist on and achieve a quality technology deployment. This works even from a self-serving perspective—it's the easiest way to achieve a string of highly successful consulting projects!

Certified Security Consultant

Recently, I was happy to see a RFP for security consulting services that stated: "Preference – the consultant has the CSC (Certified Security Consultant) designation." (For more information on this certification visit the IAPSC website at www.iapsc.org.) The CSC certification is available not only to independent consultants but also to security managers (i.e., the company's internal security consultants) who meet the qualifications.

To my thinking, any security practitioner who manages or intends to deploy hundreds of thousands or millions of dollars of physical security technology should work to achieve this certification. Being able to effectively deploy security technology can be a career maker; not being so able can be a career breaker.

Finding Security Specifiers

When you need specifications for a security system or a particular security technology, how do you find a qualified design specialist? Until recently it wasn't always easy. Now it is, thanks to SecuritySpecifiers™. I am proud to say that I'm on its consultant Board of Advisors, and I am in excellent company there. Even if you don't have an immediate need for a design and specifications consultant, or if you are a consultant and haven't been to the website, check out securityspecifiers.com today.

THE DEADLOCKING PLUNGER WEAKNESS

One recent facility security assessment started with the question below, and, after encountering this vulnerability in every assessment for the past 15 years, it became obvious that it was time to write about it. The problem is easily remedied.

> **Q: We installed a good quality lock industrial, yet someone was able to bypass it using a credit card. How could this be?**
>
> **A:** Most likely the door latch installation somehow kept the deadlocking plunger (also called a deadlock latch) from being engaged, or allowed it to be disengaged. It is the purpose of this part of the door lock mechanism to prevent doors from being opened in this fashion.

Over the past 15 years, as I tracked this particular vulnerability in our facility security assessments, in every commercial facility security assessment

I performed I found at least one door that could be easily opened (in 5 s or less) with a credit card, screwdriver, or hair comb. Facility managers have been amazed to see strong commercial and industrial locks bypassed this way. Recently, at one facility, after a big-name company installed card and pin electronic access control (card reader plus keypad) for a half-dozen critical internal doors, I was able to slip a comb out of my pocket and pop open each door. IT departments take note: This vulnerability is common for IT equipment room closets, especially where the closet originally served another purpose and was later given to IT without upgrading the door to a security-grade installation.

What is a Deadlocking Plunger?

For convenience in closing doors, many types of door latch bolts have a beveled tip shape, as shown in Figure 6.1. The purpose of the angle is to enable the latch bolt to be pushed in automatically as the door is closed; otherwise you'd have to manually twist the doorknob to retract the latch and be able to close the door. However, that feature is a security weakness. When the door is closed you can push the latch-back bolt using a screwdriver, metal ruler, plastic card, and so on, as shown in Figure 6.2.

To keep the latch bolt from being push-retractable once the door is closed, a second mechanism is incorporated into the latching mechanism: a deadlocking plunger (the entire mechanism sometimes is called a deadlock latch), as shown in Figure 6.3. When the plunger is kept pushed in by the strike plate, the latch bolt cannot retract. However, security assessments commonly find that the strike plate is the wrong type or the wrong size, allowing both the latch bolt and the deadlocking plunger to be fully extended. In such an instance, the bolt can be pushed back, as shown in Figure 6.4. Sometimes the deadlocking plunger mechanism simply doesn't work, and in my assessments about 10%

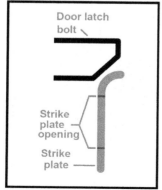

FIGURE 6.1 Note the beveled tip of the door latch bolt.

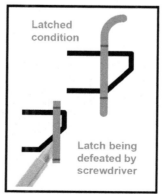

FIGURE 6.2 Latch without a deadlocking plunger being forced open with a screwdriver.

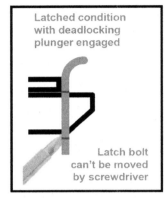

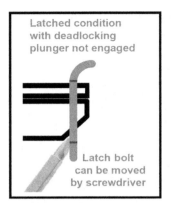

FIGURE 6.3 With the deadlocking plunger engaged, a screwdriver can exploit the beveled end of a door latch bolt.

FIGURE 6.4 If the deadlocking plunger is the wrong size or type, the bolt is still at risk of being forced open.

of the types of plunger illustrated in these figures fails. (To test, with the door open, push the plunger back and see if you can still retract the latch bolt.)

Commercial and industrial security locksets with a higher rating use an improved design. One such design can be seen in the Simplex 900 Lockset shown in Figure 6.5, in which the deadlocking plunger is separated vertically

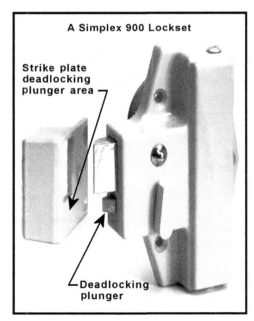

FIGURE 6.5 A Simplex 900 lockset with the deadlocking plunger separated vertically from the latch bolt.

from the latch bolt. (I am using this lockset as an example because it has a YouTube video of the lockset rotating, providing a good view of the latching mechanism: http://www.youtube.com/watch?v=Z_rWE3SxsZE/.)

If the latch is closed, there is no possibility of the deadlocking plunger being extended in a well-built and properly installed security door. An example of poor door installation is one where a crowbar can be inserted between the door and the strike plate and turned to push the strike plate away from the plunger. Once the strike plate is pushed away, the deadlocking plunger is extended, and the latch bolt can be easily pushed back.

Knowledge of these aspects of door design is well understood by most locksmiths, but not by enough security practitioners and facility managers. Good advice is to check every building perimeter door and every door leading to critical facility areas and critical assets.

SMART PROJECTS

Smart projects are projects that don't shortchange the requirements, design, and proof-of-concept testing. This reader's question shows that a smart integrator is bidding the project.

> **Q: I just received a proposal from a security integrator for a video system project with 50 total outdoor and indoor cameras that will take four to five months. My team thought it would take maybe 3 months in the worst case. We have pre-selected the cameras and video management system.** *Does this mean that the integrator doesn't have enough experience to do this kind of project?*
>
> **A:** Quite to the contrary, it most likely means that the integrator has lots of experience doing this type of project, and is taking into account that although product selection has been done, detailed requirements and design work still remain.

In this situation, it turned out that the integrator was allowing for the up-front development of requirements, a detailed design, and proof-of-concept testing (for camera lens selection and on-camera video analytics), plus a 30-day operational test at the end of the project. There was an additional allowance for turnaround time in getting customer information and approvals, given that no written functional requirements currently exist. It ended up that the part of the work that the customer envisioned really was 2–3 months, but the other 2 months of key work required for project success were not in the customer's vision.

Up-Front Design Work is Critical

On several recent video projects I learned of, once the specifics of the security operations requirements had been worked out, motion detectors had to be relocated, cameras moved, and the default lenses of some cameras replaced by wide-angle and telephoto lenses.

Today's advanced technology requires a more detailed design approach than was required in the past. In the days when only analog cameras were available, there were fewer capabilities and options for a video system. HD and multimegapixel cameras, 180° multilens cameras, on-board camera analytics, and other advanced technologies have vastly increased the number of factors involved in designing camera deployments. If you need to do more than just determine what type of activity is taking place, how detailed and clearly in focus the image is may be critically important—and that requires effectively using the right technology.

The technologies described below can increase the security-effectiveness and cost-effectiveness of video deployments, as long as the right design steps are taken initially.

Precision iris: Also known as "P-Iris," this is an automatic, precise iris control developed by Axis Communications of Sweden and the Kowa Company of Japan. It involves a P-Iris lens and specialized software in the camera that optimize image quality. P-Iris technology provides improvements in contrast, clarity, resolution, and depth of field, especially with megapixel cameras. (Download a six-page white paper about P-Iris from http://bit.ly/p-iris.)

IR-corrected lenses: IR-correction means that sharper focus is now obtainable for both standard and multimegapixel cameras. The lens IR correction focuses IR light from artificial illumination at the same plane as visible light. With normal lenses, IR light and visible light focus in different planes, resulting in either the IR image or visible light image being out of focus. This type of lens sharpens daylight images, as well nighttime images. (Download a two-page white paper about IR-corrected lenses, with diagrams and images, from http://bit.ly/ir-corrected-lens.)

Ultra-wide angle image correction: Image distortion is not a factor in the ultra-wide-angle lenses from Theia Technologies, which incorporate patented technology that optically corrects the barrel distortion typically produced by very wide-angle lenses. (For details and example images, see http://bit.ly/ultra-wide-lens.)

Video analytics: The use of video analytics, whether server-based or camera-based, requires considerable application design effort. Recorded video must be searched for examples of behavior to be detected, or example video must be created, as the starting point for design. Proof-of-concept testing using live and recorded video is required to verify the workability of analytics applications, both for reliable detection and to eliminate nuisance alarms.

Project Time

Small projects can take double the time required for legacy technology but can produce very impressive results. Allowing enough time for up-front design work, proof-of-concept testing, and operational fine-tuning will provide operational capabilities you can be proud of and that live up to the Return On Investment (ROI) potential of the technology.

SMART PERIMETER DETECTION PROJECTS

More often than not it's the process—not the technology—that is to blame for failed perimeter detection projects.

> **Q: I and my security team spent many hours examining and comparing megapixel video cameras and analytics technology and finally made selections for our fence line perimeter security project. After installation and several months of "tuning", not only are we are still getting nuisance alarms, we are also failing to detect intrusions. How can I hold the manufacturers accountable?**
>
> **A:** Unless they specifically promised you contractually to provide a perfectly working system, the most you can do is enable them to determine what role, if any, their products can have in your solution when you fix it.

The real problem lies in the technology selection and deployment process, which is the diagnosis for most failed technology projects. Unfortunately, this is a very common situation when it comes to perimeter detection projects, from small to large. The Internet contains articles recounting fence-line perimeter security projects upward of $100 million that failed miserably. But when your own project is in crisis, it's very small comfort to know that other projects have failed as well.

The only way to guarantee that such a project will be successful is to perform pilot tests in the field. That is actually what this project turned out to be: a very expensive and extremely upsetting field test. *A design is just a theoretical solution until the various design elements have been verified or proven.*

Requirements are a Critical Challenge

Detecting motion and objects is hardly ever the challenge. The challenge is reporting only the valid objects or conditions as alarms and being able to ignore the "normal" conditions that would otherwise trigger an analytics event report.

There are numerous stories of projects where cats, dogs, rabbits, ground hogs, opossums, owls, coyotes, and mountain lions turned out to be a significant source of nuisance alarms. Then there are the wind-blown newspapers and shopping bags that hit fences and stick or cross the video detection areas of cameras. Sunrise and sunset change the video image, as do headlights from passing cars outside the target area. Baseballs and basketballs can also cause problems, but those usually constitute acceptable nuisance alarms since they occur rarely and usually foreshadow an "innocent" intrusion that is the attempt to retrieve them. It is the commonly occurring potential nuisance alarms that you need to deal with most.

This is why, for this kind of project, developing the requirements is significantly more than a word-processing exercise. You have to *know for sure* what the field conditions are. That usually means temporarily installing cameras of the kind you expect to use and recording a couple of weeks of video around the clock. During this time period, you want to create multiple instances of each type of intrusion activity that you want to detect. Be sure to create each condition in three ways: at the near and far ends of the camera's field of view, as well as in the middle. Close to the camera, a dog can appear larger than a person crawling at the farthest point from the camera. Additional complicating factors are seasonal changes. Facility grounds can look very different in summer and winter. Fall leaves can calls cause problems, too.

Testing is Critical, Too

Save time and money by using laboratory testing before field testing. Now that you have recorded the video containing examples of a valid event (what you want to report as alarms) and nuisance events (what you don't want to report as alarms), give copies of the video to your candidate analytics vendors. There are server-based analytics, edge appliance-based analytics, and camera-based analytics. Testing multiple analytics products and approaches in parallel saves calendar time.

Note that providing all of the vendors with the same video clips is the only way to get a true competitive performance comparison. Vendors are usually receptive to this approach because they get to collect examples of what works well and what doesn't and can more easily avoid raising false expectations among prospective customers.

If and when you find products that perform satisfactorily, then you can perform an actual field pilot test. Pilot testing is extremely important if you are deploying the technology at many sites. In such a situation, remember that not all sites are the same, so establishing a few pilot sites rather than just one might be wise.

The pilot test is where you can closely examine the strengths and weaknesses of the products, and you should create as many activities and conditions as you can think up to "stress test" the technology and determine its boundaries of acceptable performance. Engaging an integrator to execute the pilot project gives both you and the integrator experience that will be valuable for the final deployment and for ongoing maintenance.

If you are using multiple technologies as a way to reduce false positives, expect that to increase the testing time by 50%.

This is also an approach that will be successful in fixing troubled perimeter intrusion detection projects.

BACKUP POWER FOR VIDEO SYSTEMS

There can be special considerations involved in deploying uninterruptible power supply (UPS) devices and performing an orderly shutdown upon losing main power to video system servers.

> **Q: Why did we still lose all our recorded video when we had a long power outage, even though the video server was connected to our UPS and should have performed an orderly shutdown before the UPS battery was exhausted?**
>
> **A:** The network attached storage was not also on the UPS and so was not protected from instantly being powered off upon the loss of power. Data corruption resulted.

With DVRs, at least a partial loss of recorded video upon power outages was common, unless the DVRs had UPS battery backup power and the power outages were short enough that the UPS could sustain the machines throughout the outage. Many DVR systems did not have backup power.

Unless cameras and any connecting equipment (e.g., video amplifiers or network switches) can be run off battery backup or emergency power, it makes no sense to keep video recording units—whether DVRs, NVRs, or servers—running during a power outage. There would be no video data to record. The main concern for the recording units should be to keep them powered long enough to shut them down correctly so that there is no data corruption.

PoE Makes Backup Camera Power Feasible

Powering cameras from local power sources close to the camera makes UPS backup power for camera infeasible, since providing a UPS at every camera power point would be cost prohibitive. Now, however, using PoE-powered cameras means that keeping the network switches powered automatically keeps the cameras powered. So, where maintaining video monitoring of critical asset areas is crucial, such as in health care facilities, PoE power can be an affordable solution that enables cameras, as well as their recording units, to keep functioning throughout a power outage.

All Systems Have a Risk of Data Loss

For most video systems, emergency power won't be provided during long power outages. Even where emergency backup power is available, if there is even a momentary problem, power system video servers could still lose power. Thus, for nearly all security video deployments, addressing UPS backup power and orderly shutdown for video servers and all related components is important.

Orderly Shutdown Can Be Simple or Complex

The simplest scenario for implementing orderly shutdown is a single-server computer containing the video storage hard drives, whose backup power comes from a UPS dedicated to that computer. A USB connection from the UPS to the computer provides the data interface, and software provided by the UPS manufacturer can be configured to (a) perform an orderly shutdown when a main power outage occurs and (b) ensure that the computer powers up when main power is restored. Various options exist to allow for an appropriate shutdown sequence, for example, shutting down the video management server (VMS) application, then shutting down the SQL server, then shutting down the operating systems and powering off the machine.

An example of a complex orderly shutdown scenario is one with multiple video servers and a UPS shared by IT servers as well as the video servers. The video servers are virtual machine host computers, each with several virtual machines running various applications, including the main VMS system, video analytics, SQL server, network monitoring software, and so on. The video data are written to a video SAN (storage area network). In this case the following parts of the system must be shut down in the correct order (not necessarily the order below):

- Individual applications (including the VMS) running in the virtual machines
- Instances of a SQL server running in the virtual machines
- Virtual machine operating systems
- Virtual machine host server itself
- Video SAN storage units
- Any network equipment switches and routers that connect video servers and storage servers

A UPS that supports network-based data connections from multiple computers is required, not just a one-computer USB connection. Such a UPS typically would support simple network monitoring protocol, which IT would use to monitor the status of the UPS and receive notifications about changes in power status, which could be used to trigger power outage notifications to security. Vendor-specific protocols also exist, usually for use with vendor-provided UPS management software.

The IT department would establish the shutdown and restart configurations for the IT servers on the UPS. Be sure to establish logging with real-time error notification for the shutdown sequence so that contingencies for video outage can be activated and any errors can be identified and corrected, allowing quick manual intervention in the event of a significant shutdown error.

Orderly Startup is Also Required

An orderly startup sequence is required when power is restored, which may or may not be the reverse sequence of the shutdown. Startup times will be different than shutdown times, and startup operations should also be logged with real-time notification.

Design for Sufficient Shutdown Time

In a complex system the shutdown time may be 30 min or longer, depending on the shutdown sequences required and how much time each individual application and operating system requires to perform its orderly shutdown. This may exceed the requirements of other UPS users in the data center, equipment rack, or room where the equipment is located.

Large hard disk storage arrays, whether inside the server computer or in a separate storage system, can use up a great deal of battery backup power. This means that accurately calculating total UPS load and battery-backed uptime for the systems is very important. Fortunately, once the UPS battery is fully charged, the software provided with the UPS will report the estimated battery time for the connected load.

The UPS must be able to support the total duration of time required for the full shutdown sequence, including a good margin of safety for shutdown time. Error logging and notification add more time to the overall shutdown process. Both the full shutdown sequence and startup sequence must be tested and timed, including notifications.

Protect Your Video System Investment

Find out what brand and model of UPS your IT department uses as a standard; using that brand can put IT in the position of easily providing you with design and implementation support. A popular product line is the APC SMARTUPS 1500 series, which supports a single USB data connection as a standard but also has a network add-in card option to support multiple computers. If the video recording is performed in a corporate data center, there may be access to high-availability power from a central UPS or even a backup generator.

When attending a security trade show, take data about your VMS deployment (current or planned) to the show floor and ask your VMS vendor or candidate vendors how they would recommend you establish orderly shutdown and restart of all the server components of your system. Request an application note, white paper, or specific written guidance; *they should have such materials available*.

Your security video system is a significant investment. Don't allow power outages to destroy recorded video or corrupt server operating system files, when a good UPS system can prevent such problems for a fraction of the cost of the total system.

UPS INTEGRATION FOR VIDEO

For video servers, there are special considerations regarding UPS support and establishing an orderly shutdown before and orderly startup after a power outage. This section follows up on the previous section, "Backup Power for Video Systems."

> **Q: Our security systems integrator installed a two-hour UPS for our video servers, but when a 4-hour power failure occurred, the server did not come back on. Why not?**
>
> **A:** There is much more involved in UPS support than physically installing a UPS and plugging the video servers' power cables into it.

Typically, video recording servers are not provided with emergency power because (until the advent of PoE cameras) emergency power could not easily be provided to cameras during a power outage. Keeping the recording system powered up if the cameras are powered down makes no sense.

Ignoring the impact of a power outage on a video server can be catastrophic, however, because a hard shutdown can leave the video data in a corrupted state. Even if a video server powers back up without any apparent issues, a corrupted video database may not properly store data going forward, and a significant amount of previously recorded video can be lost, as well. Such problems are typically detected only during an investigation, when the full extent of the video loss is discovered.

This is why providing *and properly integrating* a UPS is critically important. A video server with terabytes or petabytes of redundant array of independent disks hard drive storage can be protected with just ~10 min of UPS power—just enough power to allow the video management software, the operating system, and the storage expansion servers to shut down in the correct sequence. If the storage expansion servers are powered down before the video server they support, data corruption can result. If there is a network switch between the primary video server and its expansion storage, the switch must remain powered on until both servers have shut down.

The shutdown sequence should be something like this for a video server with an expansion storage unit, to which it communicates via a network switch:

1. *VMS software*. The VMS software should be shut down first, which may involve shutting down one or more VMS components running as operating system services. The VMS has to stop writing to the hard drives before any storage expansion units can be shut down.
2. *Server operating system*. Once the VMS has been shut down, the operating system can be shut down.
3. *Storage expansion units*. Once the video server operating system has been shut down, storage expansion units can be shut down.
4. *Network switch*. If there is a network switch between the VMS server and the storage units, that switch may now be shut down. Typically, network switches are left running and will either shut down when the UPS turns off or remain running throughout the outage.

The startup sequence should work in the *reverse* order. For example, if the network switch is not running, the server and its storage expansion units can't communicate. If the VMS tries to record data and the storage expansion unit is not yet up and running, the VMS will encounter errors writing to the data files and/or database, which may require manual intervention to establish correct operation.

Integrating to the UPS Device

The right kind of UPS device comes with documented software on a disk that can be installed on Windows or Linux servers and used to communicate with the UPS via a network or USB connection. Where multiple servers or storage units are powered by the same UPS, the UPS will require multiport network cards, which is usually an optional item.

Once the UPS notifies the servers integrated with it that power has been lost, the shutdown sequence should be initiated. Sometimes it takes a bit of testing to discover the worst-case timing requirements for each element that has to be shut down or started up as part of a sequence.

It's usually very expensive in terms of UPS battery cost to provide the capability to keep many terabytes or more of video hard drives running throughout a power outage. With PoE power available, however, nowadays putting some of the camera-connected segments of the video network on emergency or backup power to enable critical cameras to record to secure digital memory cards during a power outage is feasible. This is easier to do in environments where uninterrupted power is a high requirement, such as in health care facilities.

Your video project should always include a power plan, and the use of emergency and UPS power should be a part of that plan. If this subject is unfamiliar to you, it's likely that your IT group will have one or more subject matter experts on power provision for critical IT systems. A security design consultant worth his or her salt will be able to help you with this, as well.

CHAPTER 7

Standards Convergence

This chapter's material includes four different types of standards—all of which have a common factor: In any organization they are usually applied or used within either the physical security or information technology (IT) group, but not in both. Chances are they are all topics worth a collaborative discussion in your organization.

STANDARDS CAN PROVIDE SIGNIFICANT BENEFITS

The subject of standards is worthy of attention. Two categories of standards are external and internal. External standards are developed outside your organization by official standards bodies or arise as de-facto standards for an industry or profession. Organizations select or apply them based on their requirements and objectives. Internal standards are developed by an organization's own personnel, also based on requirements and objectives. Standards establish minimum levels of quality; provide economies in training, installation, service, and support; and ensure that devices and systems can work together. Thus IT departments have long used internal standards for corporate computers and networks. This is something generally lacking for corporate physical security systems.

Some internal standards are standards of practice, which simply means having a specific way of doing things to ensure correctness and completeness. These are often documented as named procedures or standard operating procedures, or job aids, which are instructions on how to do a particular task.

Because physical security's electronic systems are based on IT (computers, networks, software, databases, wireless communication, analytics, and so on), security managers can benefit by applying internal IT expertise to their physical security systems. This is illustrated by the answers below.

Q: What are some of the ways that you have been able to leverage IT expertise for physical security and what were the benefits?

A: Preparing for a complete upgrade of our physical security systems (encompassing several counties), we asked IT to consult with us in regards to the network and computer aspects of our upgrade. All of our existing systems were independent at each facility. The IT personnel asked us questions about computers and operating systems, network traffic priority, network quality of service, and the type of network traffic our systems would have. We didn't know about those things, so IT assigned us a person full time to work with us on these and other issues. We reviewed the existing IT standards and found a number of items, such as daily operating systems patches for servers, which were not workable for a security system. Nor would it be acceptable for security system communications to be interrupted for an evening or weekend for network maintenance. We learned that we could employ a staging platform (extra set of servers) to test operating system and software upgrades, before applying them to our in-service systems. We learned that IT could prioritize certain types of security traffic that would go over business network segments, to ensure that security system communications would not be bumped out by other less critical systems. To utilize the business network backbone (wide area network), our security network would have to utilize specific equipment for its connections to the WAN. We would also have to employ computer and network security. These things went into a new IT standards document for our security systems and networks. We provided this standard to bidding integrators. Our networking of systems went without any major hitches. We didn't lose any project time because we addressed these issues in advance. Our security systems and networks are highly secure, are also compatible with the future plans of our IT department as well as our planned system expansion. We know that what we have installed is a very good value for our money spent.

—Security Project Manager, Major Public Utility

A: After realizing that we had been deploying security computers and networks without having any IT expertise in our security department, we decided to appoint a technology specialist in our group and invite IT to examine our systems and share any of their thoughts with him. We learned a lot. For example, we bought DVRs early on, without fully realizing that the DVR box contained a computer running Windows, and that computer expertise would be required to set up and maintain it. Our DVRs were set up with only one large hard drive, and both the operating system and the video recording were being performed on to the same drive. If the hard drive failed, we would lose all of the machine's recorded video and all of the configuration data (we didn't have a backup scheme in place). This design overworked the single hard drive's internal mechanisms, because the drive would have to switch back and forth between spots on the drive's disks to swap between writing video data and writing operating system data. The recommendation from IT was to add additional drives in a RAID configuration, so that if we lost one drive we could simply replace it with a new drive and continue on without any loss of existing data. By having separate drives for the operating system and for video recording, the life of the drives would be extended because they would not be overworked. This is now part of the new technology standards we are developing.

—Security Manager, Major Manufacturing Company

LESSONS LEARNED: PHYSICAL SECURITY AND IT COLLABORATION

In the past few years, many companies have initiated active collaboration between the physical security and IT groups. As one physical security manager from a major software company said to me recently, "Convergence is not a new thing for us. Convergence just means working together. Our IT guys don't even like the word because it makes it sound like some kind of outside force is at work. At our company convergence started long before it was popular in the industry because the IT folks wanted to help us out in any way that they could. Our collaboration with IT was driven by forces inside the company, people who think—correctly so—that it's just a part of their job. It was a natural thing for us."

This company's corporate culture has always had a strong "let's work together" element that naturally led to collaboration between physical security and IT. Since the majority of the company's personnel are IT people, there was also a much larger pool of talent to draw from. Not all companies are in that situation, but all companies can benefit from their simple perspective: convergence means working together.

Enough companies have established successful collaborations between their physical security and IT departments that it was possible to collect a number of their convergence "tips" or "lessons learned." These will be presented in the next few sections. Here, the answer is a combination of responses from a number of companies.

Q: What tips, recommendations or lessons learned would you share with other companies who want to establish collaboration between their physical security and IT groups?

A: It has been very beneficial for many companies to establish company standards for the IT elements of physical security systems. These are "preapproved" and are applied to any security systems project. Establishing standards required a lot of thought and time up front but subsequently saved a lot of time and effort. Now with each security project these elements don't have to be "figured out" each time from a blank sheet. Projects start by determining how the standards apply and go forward quickly. In budget proposals the standards-based elements of implementations are identified, and that approach has lessened the concern over what is being done technically.

Here are the categories of standards that have been developed for physical security systems:

- Computer servers and workstations
- Network storage systems
- Network routers, switches and firewalls
- Network naming conventions
- IP addressing
- Network Quality of Service (QoS)
- Network protocol requirements
- Computer use security policy (including requirements related to passwords and logons)
- System maintenance policy (such as operating system patching requirements)
- Remote access policy (dial-up or network access for technical support, or home access)
- Use of antivirus and other computer security software
- Equipment closets and communication rooms
- Forensics requirements (such as audit trails and computer security incident response)
- System backup and recovery policy
- Change management
- System design documentation requirements
- Acceptance testing
- Business Continuity Planning

For example, network protocol requirements include SNMP (simple network management protocol) and NTP (network time protocol). Network Quality of Service requirements include identifying video camera pan-tilt-zoom (PTZ) control traffic as high priority traffic. Business Continuity Planning involves identifying how the existing planning will be extended to incorporate the new security system elements. The IT group has dealt with all of these issues for their own systems, so in most cases only a little bit of work is needed to establish the standards for physical security systems. In some cases it is simply enough to reference an existing IT standard, such as network naming conventions, and apply it as it is. One company found that the IT department didn't have an established standard for some items, but their development was on IT's "to do" list. Physical security then participated in the overall IT standards development effort for those items.

A: Our initial meetings were very awkward for us, because the IT personnel had a lot of questions that we couldn't answer. They had to spend a lot of time explaining things to us, and our collaboration efforts fizzled initially because we just didn't feel comfortable, and in retrospect I think we didn't have specific enough objectives for our discussions. A security colleague of mine at another company suggested that we identify a potential project that would involve IT, and have an exploratory discussion with them about that. We had been considering integration between our physical access control system (PACS) with the HR system. We collaborated with our vendor and system integrator to write a description of what we wanted to accomplish, and why, and sent that by email with a request for a telephone conference. During the conference, our vendor's tech specialist and our integrator's IT specialist took the lead, and that was a highly productive call.

Once the IT guys discovered they were talking to people with IT knowledge and project experience, communication started flowing and we covered all kinds of bases. We learned about some corporate privacy restrictions covering the data that we wanted to access, including special restrictions on employee home telephone numbers. Those were not needed for the PACS integration, but we did want to have access to them for emergency notification situations. Some corporate policies had been established with regard to privacy training regarding access to privacy-restricted data, and our type of application hadn't been considered when those policies were developed. Following up on the application of privacy policies was one of several action items that resulted from our conference call.

It turned out that a few years earlier the company had undergone an effort to consolidate many of its databases, especially those that were personnel related, to eliminate duplicate information and weed out inaccurate data. We were surprised that the employee name information on our security badges wasn't taken into account. It turned out that it had been assumed that the information came from an HR database. So in a sense our integration project could be considered an extension of the original company project, at least in terms of its purpose.

One of the side effects of this collaboration—and this was in large part due to the expertise that our vendor and integrator brought to the table and the rapport they established with the IT personnel—was that some of the IT folks began to champion our project initiatives within IT and also at corporate planning meetings. We followed through on the initial conference call by having additional conference calls with our vendor and integrator to have them provide us with some education on the various IT issues that were discussed. Now we have several people in our Security Department who can productively discuss related issues with IT.

I think the key success factors for us were (a) having something specific to discuss even if exploratory, (b) having people with IT expertise involved in our initial discussions, and (c) following up to make sure that the appropriate Security Department personnel got educated on the specific IT issues that were related to our projects. We didn't spend anywhere near as much time on all this as we thought we might, and the time was consistently very productive.

—Security Manager, Global Manufacturing Company

SINGLE LOGICAL/PHYSICAL ACCESS CARD STANDARDS

Expanding information security requirements are prompting IT departments to implement stronger logical access control to critical systems and networks, especially for remote workers (such as those traveling or working from home). Independently, some corporate security departments are considering upgrading outdated legacy PACSs to current technology. Often, this prompts questions, such as the one below, about using a single card for both physical and logical access and as a corporate photo identification badge, as well.

> **Q: We'd like to approach IT about using a single smart card for physical and logical access control. I have read that some companies like Boeing, Microsoft and Sun Microsystems have implemented a single card for physical and logical access. We know that the U.S. federal government has issued the FIPS 201 standard for government use for combined physical and logical access on a smart card. Are there any standards for private companies?**

> **A:** Many companies are now looking to upgrade the levels of assurance for their logical and physical access control. FIPS 201 is the U.S. federal government standard that specifies Personal Identity Verification (PIV) requirements for Federal employees and contractors. The set of FIPS 201 related standards has been expanded, and there are now two additional standards for cards issued by private sector organizations: PIV-Interoperable (PIV-I for short) and PIV Compatible (PIV-C). The Smart Card Alliance (www.smartcardalliance.org) provides a wealth of information for private sector application of PIV requirements that includes standards, case studies, technology announcements, and notes on applications in specific business sectors. Detailed information can be found on the Smart Card Alliance website.

> In particular, take a look at this page: http://tinyurl.com/smart-cards-for-enterprise-id. This page provides many document download links about the use of smart cards for physical and logical access in non-government settings.

The Key Factor Is Establishing Trust

Between people, high degrees of trust are established by successful interaction or performance over a period of time, and by association; for example, someone we trust recommends or vouches for another person *for a specific purpose and in a specific context*. Thus there are different levels of trust required for different situations, and different levels of assurance. You would select a heart surgeon in the context of his or her surgical practice and an association with a particular hospital. You know that the hospital has performed a high level of background checks before allowing the surgeon to practice. You may check some references on your own. This is not a 15-min process and could be longer than a 15-day process. You may select a house painter through a contractor referral service. That may be a 15-min process or quicker. For this reason, FIPS 201 and related standards do address varying levels of assurance.

A Trusted Credential

For electronic access control—whether for computers and networks or for facilities and physical building areas—we use an electronic credential of one kind or another. This can be a photo badge, a name and password, or something more. We substitute recognizing the credential for recognizing the person, which means two important things. First, the process of issuing the credential must include verification of the person's identity through some trusted approach (such as birth certificates, driver licenses, and so on). Second, the credential is bound to the person through one or more biometric associations. Typically, this has been through a printed name and photo on an access card or badge. With smart cards, this can include a biometric signature (scan of fingerprint, retina, hand geometry, vein pattern, and so on) that is stored on the card. Data on the card can be stored and retrieved using information security technology that guards against forgery, alteration, and misuse of the card. With that in place we have a situation in which we have a high level of identity assurance in the use of the credential.

Are You Who You Say You Are?

If a highly trusted technology produces a card that is issued through a process with weak identify verification, what use is the advanced technology? The card could be issued to the wrong person. This is a situation that the FIPS 201 PIV requirements address, and they do so through defining requirements (including roles and responsibilities) for three key processes:

1. Identity proofing and registration
2. Card issuance and maintenance
3. Access control

An excellent introduction to these processes and other aspects of PIV requirements is found in a white paper "Important FIPS 201 Deployment Considerations," produced by CoreStreet, which you can download from: http://tinyurl.com/FIPS-201-Key-Considerations. Note that card *personalization* (a term used in the white paper) refers to the process of printing the photo and other information on the smart card and encoding electronic information specific to the cardholder.

If you are not familiar with the specifics of FIPS 201 and PIV, this white paper is a good place to start. Follow that by identifying relevant information from the Smart Card Alliance website. This information can help get corporate security and IT security walking down the same path.

WHERE DO STANDARDS LEAD?

Physical security technology has advanced (and changed) considerably in the past 15 years. Yet most end users of security technology take the same approach to technology deployment that they did 15 or more years ago. If we want to advance the results we get from security technology (as opposed to simply getting the same results for a lower cost), we have to advance our thinking. This is the issue behind the following question from an end user.

> **Q: At the ASIS Annual Seminar and Exhibits I saw demonstrations of products that are compliant with the new Physical Security Interoperability Alliance (PSIA) and Open Network Video Interface Forum (ONVIF) interoperability standards. Since these products included the brands that I already use and plan to keep using, what actual benefit do the interoperability standards provide to me?**
>
> **A:** There are many values to be obtained from the adoption of interoperability standards, and most of these have been written about or analyzed in security industry trade journals, and online articles and blogs. However, to make sure that you benefit fully from standards adoption in the industry requires that you take a modern-day approach to security technology deployment. This can require a significant change in thinking … one that includes the concept of "evolvable infrastructure".

Where Interoperability Standards Lead

Wikipedia (http://en.wikipedia.org/wiki/Infrastructure) has an excellent article on the topic of "infrastructure," and many of the concepts relate to the benefits of establishing a security technology infrastructure. An evolvable technology infrastructure is the opposite of what has been the most common approach to security technology deployment, which was *purchase, maintain, then rip and replace*. This was suitable when product life cycles were 10–15 years and when the pace of technology advancement could be monitored easily by attending a trade show every 4 or 5 years. Now technology advancements occur as frequently as every 6 months. Not only are annual rip-and-replace cycles not affordable, they are also not necessary to keep pace with technology advances. Interoperability among networked devices means that it is now becoming possible to establish an infrastructure whose capabilities can be continually improved as technology advances occur. The appropriate way to approach security technology deployment is to establish an evolvable security technology infrastructure, which I define as:

> A managed network of electronic security systems and devices that is configured, operated, maintained, and continually enhanced to provide security functions and services that achieve specific security risk mitigation objectives.

The following diagram illustrates the evolution from standalone products and systems to achieving a standards-based evolvable infrastructure.

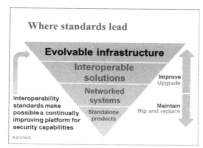

For a closer look at what the concept of an evolvable infrastructure means, view the online webinar titled "The Road to Interoperable IP Solutions" (available at: www.psialliance.org/PSIAWebinars.html; original broadcast, September 22, 2010).

One of the most important benefits of adopting interoperability standards is that it makes possible the continual improvement of security technology deployments so that security operations capabilities can evolve as business environments and risk profiles evolve.

STRATEGIC MATCH-UP

Many security technology convergence collaborations come about as a specific need or specific project. For example, there is a need to share video with stakeholders across the network, and consequently discussions are begun between security operations and IT about how to accomplish that. This is one of the more simple examples, although even seemingly simple situations can turn out to be complicated based on the bigger picture, as the question below illustrates. Roadmap planning can provide a larger context for additional complexities and turn a "problem-solving" situation into a successful planning initiative.

> **Q: I have a need to provide access to live and recorded video to some of our real estate people. I approached IT, explaining that we wanted to implement Quality of Service (QoS) protocols (I understand this could be important on a high-traffic network) to ensure that the video on the**

viewing end would be smooth and not jumpy or jittery, or not have empty squares in parts of the image (this happened with one webcam we put up quickly to watch some emergency construction work). IT said "No" because QoS was further down their roadmap. Should I think about trying to convince them to change their roadmap, or do I try instead to get funding for a separate network run?

—Security Operations Manager

A: There is more than one way to address network traffic integrity, and an IT-savvy technician from your integrator, or an independent technology consultant, can explain the options based upon the current state of your corporate network. However, this situation highlights the need for high-level collaboration. Unless security's technology roadmap and IT's technology roadmap are in alignment, after solving this issue subsequent attempts at collaboration could be challenging, just like this one. IT shouldn't change their long-term roadmap based upon a single need or one-off solution request. However, it is the role of IT to anticipate and serve the organization's long-term network needs, and if these can be presented by any functional area or business unit, that may provide IT with sufficient reason to expand or adjust the roadmap. Alternatively, IT's plan may be an excellent one and, if already funded, it may be appropriate for security to schedule its technology improvements in a way that matches up with the network infrastructure work being done by IT.

Technology Roadmaps

Technology roadmap development should start with identifying the business needs and functions to be supported. For example, when one company wanted to implement flex time for its employees, arriving early during some portions of the year meant arriving before sunrise. Additional security lighting was needed along some paths in the facility complex. Some buildings that didn't have video cameras and intercoms at their main doors would now need them to enable employees to contact security if they had forgotten their access card or if a security concern arose.

Because security participated in the business's change management process, these needs were identified ahead of time. IP intercoms were considered to be the most cost-effective way to add intercoms. Establishing QoS on the network paths for the intercoms was important to ensure voice-quality sound. IT already had a QoS rollout planned as part of its larger voice over IP (VOIP) telephone project, and so the QoS implementation for intercoms (being done ahead of the VOIP initiative) would need to meet the standards set for the VOIP initiative. All of the other business changes needed were identified, planned and budgeted, and rolled out according to an overall schedule. During discussions, security mentioned its intention to add a few outdoor network cameras, which opened more general discussions about networked video and its QoS and bandwidth requirements.

Note that many companies take the approach of "QoS by overprovisioning," which means that they provide excess network capacity so that no bottlenecks occur.

Security and IT worked together to update their technology roadmaps to be consistent with each other's plans. In this particular case security had to create a roadmap, with some guidance from IT, because security hadn't been using technology roadmaps as a planning tool in the past. It was easier than usual to get funding for the security technology upgrades because the security planning was tied in with business needs, and the timing of the funding was linked to the timing of the IT roadmap.

In this case, which I've been using as an example, the IT department was pretty savvy and included technical training for their personnel as part of their road-map. They also identified key points at which they wanted to engage specialists in network planning and design work. Security was able to get a couple of its people involved in the training and the network planning and design sessions, and in essence got professional network design consulting "free" because IT paid for the consultations.

Although this particular company didn't think of this collaboration as "con-vergence thinking" or "convergence planning," that's exactly what they were engaged in, much to the benefit of both groups.

CHAPTER 8

Convergence Initiatives

The five topics presented in this chapter are about high-benefit projects. It is likely that at least two will apply to your organization.

BENEFITS OF ACCESS CARD CONVERGENCE

Information technology (IT) continues to advance the capabilities of electronic security systems. A side effect of technological advancement is a greater focus on technology and a lesser focus on the people and process aspects of security. I asked the following question to get some feedback on some operational benefits of convergence.

Q: How has implementing a single access card for physical and IT security affected your security operations?

A: One surprise for us was the reduction—to practically zero—of security cards being reported as lost. We have always had a fair number of lost cards regardless of actions we would take to lower the number. Now that our personnel need the card to access their computers, the card itself is suddenly much more important. It's one thing to have to ask the parking attendant to raise the gate manually. It's another thing to have to tell your boss you can't answer his email until you take a few hours to replace the security card you misplaced. Had we anticipated this one benefit alone, we would have pushed for an earlier start to our single card initiative.

—**Corporate Security Director, Major International Pharmaceutical Company**

A: As part of our initiative, we made personnel access reports available to managers and supervisors. Integration with our ID management system database allows us to restrict reporting to the personnel who are under the direct supervision of the manager. Learning where people have been going when made supervisors realize that tightening up the access control privileges would eliminate employee "wandering", which is what we call it when employees are found outside of areas that concern their own work. It's not an issue of security being compromised, but the fact that distractions and superfluous activities can be eliminated by providing access privileges that are more directly related to the organizational roles of the personnel. We expect this to result in at least somewhat higher productivity, an unexpected return on investment (ROI) from our single card initiative.

—VP Physical Security, Global Financial Services Organization

A: By requiring that employees physically card into a room before they can log on to a computer there, we have eliminated physical access control tailgating. Our muster reports are now accurate for the first time, including for our senior executives and key personnel, which has been a long-time objective.

—Corporate Security Director, Global IT Services Firm

SECURITY CAMERAS FOR BUSINESS OPERATIONS USE

A side effect of technological advancement is a greater focus on technology and a lesser focus on the people and process aspects of security. I asked the question below to get feedback on some operational benefits of convergence.

Many of the responses about nonsecurity use of digital video had a common thread: quality. The first three responses below were among them. It is an interesting partnership between security and quality: both are involved in safeguarding the business by protecting assets and processes and, ultimately, protecting revenue. The fourth response, even though it is, technically speaking, a security use of video, was implemented as a cost reduction for a security process, and cost reduction was an overall business objective for the company.

Q: How has providing video access for business operations use affected your organization?

A: Our switch to digital video recording made it simple for us to provide video to production managers and supervisors. Quality is an extremely important element of our processes. Naturally, that means it is important for employees to follow both safety and quality procedures in each production line. Our first recorded major violation was met with a dismissal. Now the line employees know that they are being supervised even when the immediate supervisor is busy. We haven't had any major violations since then.

—Security Manager, Major Pharmaceutical Manufacturer

A: Watching and reviewing video we found that even in cases where the employee injury or quality event resulted from a violation of policy or procedure, we saw how we could change the systems to prevent such occurrences regardless. We originally thought that we would integrate the video clips in our training program, which we have done, to help improve employee behavior. But the long term result is more than employee awareness and improved behavior. We are actually able to make our systems safer and stronger, a benefit that we had not anticipated.

—Operations Manager, Chemical Manufacturing Facility

A: Our regional supervisors monitor store operations remotely via the security video. How well or poorly the morning and lunch peak period customers are handled has a significant impact on future business. It is expensive to recover from lowered levels of business due to poor service. Before we had the video cameras installed, we could not accurately tell whether shortcomings in service (and resultant complaints) were caused by understaffing or underperformance. Now we can see what's happening in real time and suggest ways to endear the customers to us even when a store is caught understaffed and our personnel are doing their best. Complaints are down generally and for several stores business is significantly up. Due to promotional factors, it's hard to quantify the exact impact of the remote management and supervision capability, but there is no question about its positive impact. It is a better ROI than we expected for what was originally considered primarily a security investment.

—Co-Owner, Sandwich Shop Retail Chain

A: We have chain of custody procedures instituted for certain critical materials as well as for highly confidential documentation. Prior to the introduction of security video, our risk manager required auditors to directly observe a certain percentage of materials and documentation handling and chain of custody procedures, an inherently inefficient and time-consuming process. Now an auditor can review recorded video transactions, and can check every log book entry against the recorded video. We can achieve 100% auditor coverage for monitored areas using a fraction of the manpower that was previously required. We are now requesting 100% video coverage for all critical areas. Not only does it reduce security risk, it reduces audit costs and makes it possible to fully monitor compliance.

—VP Operations, National Manufacturing Company

SHARING SECURITY TECHNOLOGY WITH BUSINESS UNITS

One aspect of the convergence of IT into physical security systems is that the systems are networkable and their data can be much more easily shared. Sharing security technology for nonsecurity business purposes increases the ROI from the security technology investment. This is especially true for video, which can provide a number of benefits for supervisory, quality, and safety personnel. Sharing security technology outside the security department adds new elements to the picture, and as a result more than technology can and should be shared.

Q: What lessons have you learned from sharing security technology with other departments?

A: We have been sharing video with manufacturing, and have learned several lessons. First of all, the training on the use of the system was not identical to our training. Most of our security officers arrived on the job familiar with pan-tilt-zoom (PTZ) control, and with nuances such as zooming in to improve the picture if a glaring light was on the periphery of the field of view. We also had to publish (and get management approval for) an acceptable use policy for video. Material along that line was included in our security officer training, but we had to break it out as a separate document, and expand it after discussions with HR and Legal about privacy concerns, etc. We had to work out a means to audit video use outside the security department to make sure that the acceptable use policy is being followed. (The old maxim applies about not issuing a policy you can't enforce.) We had to upgrade our video software to obtain a more detailed log of operator activity, to enable spot-check audits, and to review the activity of personnel when they were first given video privileges. We also had to establish secure departmental storage in each area for video exported to disc, in order to enforce our video retention policy and video access policy. These things all required more thought, and more time, then we expected would be involved in sharing the video. The most important lesson was to capture the initial enthusiasm and benefits in writing early on, as each person is given access to video. This was important for documenting the value of our initiative. Currently we are working on a way to automate metrics for man-hours saved. Since managers are busy people they don't waste time on video, but do use it to save time for supervisory and investigative purposes. Establishing a formula for manager time saved per minute of video usage, would provide a helpful metric showing the continued ROI.

—Security Manager, Manufacturer

A: Collaborating with IT was very important. We had to establish a Virtual Private Network to ensure that video stream data packets would be sent only where they needed to go on the network, and also to support network security of the video data, and to ensure quality of service over the network for all traffic during times of heavy video use. The IT department figured all of these things out in advance, and our deployment went very smoothly.

—Director of Safety & Security, Engineering Company

AUTOMATED WORKFORCE MANAGEMENT

Tough economic conditions can have an impact on businesses large and small. While not all companies are faced with workforce reduction, "doing more with less" is a nearly universal requirement in times of economic hardship.

Q: What technologies can help during tough economic times?

A: Harnessing physical access systems to support workforce management applications is the best example of how convergence of security and business apps brings bottom line improvements to the business. It turns the physical security infrastructure into a labor productivity tool and makes the security investment a source of savings, not expense. That's important at any point in the economic cycle, but it's especially popular in a recession.

—Christopher Laibe, CEO, inFRONT (www.infrontusa.com)

A: One particularly pertinent solution is an automated time and attendance system. Automated workforce management systems benefit businesses financially by eliminating common payroll errors and oversights, reducing unauthorized overtime expenses, and providing comprehensive reporting on labor dollars. In fact, most businesses utilizing automated time and attendance software experience a return on investment within three to six months of putting the system into place, with ongoing annual savings. Additionally, workforce management systems benefit the operational side of businesses by allowing the optimization of a lean workforce through improved labor allocation, enhanced scheduling solutions, and in-depth reporting.

—Erin Hagget, ITR (www.itr.ca)

After reading a white paper written by Erin Haggett titled, "Automated Workforce Management Systems: Helping Businesses Cope in Tough Economic Times" (available on the company website at http://www.itr.ca/resources-whitepapers.html), and having some discussion with Chris Laibe, President of inFRONT USA, I got a better perspective on the benefits of workforce management.

In the late 1980s—which is when I first began working with automated time and attendance—in most cases the functionality simply consisted of transferring "in" and "out" events for specific readers of an access control system. This data provided an electronic time clock function, which had a number of advantages over card-punch time clocks. For most projects that I was involved in back then, a key advantage for personnel was that any number of readers could be used for the clock-in or -out function, including existing door control readers. Most designs eliminated typical time clock queues and, of course, did away with the labor involved in managing punch cards, not to mention eliminating "buddy punching," (when a person punches in for a late or absent colleague) problems with late or early punches, and so on.

Today's systems go far beyond what the early systems provided, including web-based self-service and the automation of approval workflow for time off requests and vacation scheduling. Both the ITR and the inFRONT websites have ROI calculators that can be used to get a preliminary "take" on whether such a solution is worth evaluating.

Not all companies have such applications in place, and some companies simply export their clock-in and -out data to the payroll system, without any of the advantages that workflow management software can provide. It is definitely one way to extend the value of access control technology, especially now.

WIRELESS ANALOG OPENS VULNERABILITY

Nondigital keyboards, headsets, and microphones can create an easy hole for eavesdroppers to listen in on corporate secrets. The analog-to-digital transition has obviously been a hot topic in the security industry for several years. Below is a situation where not moving from analog to digital can have serious security impacts.

> **Q: During a recent training meeting, I noticed that the meeting room's wireless microphone system had frequencies listed on the equipment. Doesn't this mean that someone could buy a matching receiver and listen in on our meetings?**
>
> **A:** If the system is typical analog technology, the answer is yes.

Analog wireless microphones, headsets, and keyboards are all subject to eavesdropping attacks that can be accomplished with less than $100 worth of equipment. Search YouTube or the Internet and you will find countless examples and guides. Wireless vulnerabilities are easy to exploit because it can usually be done from outside the building.

If there has been no recent security assessment of meeting rooms and executive offices, and no survey of employee desktop equipment, performing one as soon as possible would be a wise move. This might be combined physical security/IT collaboration, since for any sizeable organization the most likely available resource for desktop inspection is the team of patrolling security officers. An alternative would be to have business unit managers perform checks in their own areas.

Wireless Keyboards
Analog wireless keyboards broadcast every keystroke typed, which of course includes passwords, security phrases, account numbers, and other private and sensitive data. This kind of snooping is rarely detected because it does not require any additional equipment to be plugged into the computer.

Wireless Headsets
An extremely vulnerable situation is an analog wireless headset that is "on" all the time. Sitting on the desk or hanging on the display monitor, it acts as a broadcasting microphone, transmitting conversations outside the office and building walls.

A broad spectrum of data is vulnerable within office and meeting room transmissions, including meeting participants, travel schedules, and other information that can enable physical access breaches via social engineering.

Wireless Microphones

A good wireless microphone system requires pairing each microphone to the base station using a unique electronic serial number. Simultaneous physical access to both devices should be needed to pair the two. Some systems provide optional software for use in configuring advanced features, requiring you to put the base station on the network. For security reasons, be sure to take the base station off the network when configuration is completed.

Ideally, a wireless microphone system would allow the microphone's transmission distance to be adjusted to confine it within a room or only a few feet beyond. Reducing transmission distance also helps to eliminate interference between devices when multiple systems are used in the same building.

Once the security features are in place, be sure to check the audio quality provided by the microphone system. There are wireless systems today that provide the same audio quality as wired microphones. Wireless microphones must be physically inspected periodically to make sure that the devices have the same serial numbers as those originally installed. Clever eavesdroppers can drop an extra same-brand microphone into the room—or replace an existing one—to listen in. Typically, meeting room users trying the rogue microphone would think it is broken and simply switch to a different microphone. If the microphone trouble is actually reported, it is usually after the meeting—and any eavesdropping session—are concluded.

Security Policies

Starting around 2008, wireless keyboard and headset manufacturers began switching to secure digital technology. When upgrading from analog wireless systems to digital, look for technology that supports AES 256-bit encryption, which is the standard for many government agencies and is appropriate for executive meeting rooms. Still, a number of organizations specifically forbid the use of wireless keyboards, analog headsets, and microphones. Many IT departments have specific wireless products on their acceptable products list and prohibit the use of others. *Which situation is your company in?*

CHAPTER 9

Managing Networked Technology Deployments

Technology convergence topics are not limited to system design and equipment selection. There are many aspects of managing technology deployments that are affected by convergence. In some cases it involves managing additional complexity. In other cases the convergence benefits include simplicity and greater manageability.

RESPONSIBLE DISCLOSURE AND PHYSICAL SECURITY RISK

Chapter 2 discussed vulnerability disclosures and security researchers, a discussion that focused on physical security industry products. As buildings become more automated, however, their control systems (such as lighting; heating, ventilation, and air conditioning; facility access; intrusion detection; electronic signage; and landscape irrigation) use the same network infrastructure to enable interoperability of systems, and along with the tremendous operational benefits come additional security and safety concerns.

> **Q: Why is information technology (IT) asking me, the facility security manager, about the kinds of notifications that I'd like to get? I understand that IT wants to know about my systems that I put on the network. Why would I want to know about IT systems or networks?**
>
> **A:** Responsible disclosure allows systems managers to put temporary countermeasures in place until permanent fixes can be applied. But such disclosures also provide inspiration for updating the threat model and response scenarios. So it's not just incident notification that is needed, but sharing of vulnerability identification in a way that lets threat models and response scenarios be updated appropriately.

Would you schedule a fire drill that put people in a landscaped area at the same time when the lawn and garden sprinklers are set to go off? Of course not. But suppose a disgruntled former employee or contractor took control of building systems and forced a night-time evacuation into areas where all lighting has been shut off and the grounds had been overwatered. Injuries could occur, in addition to lost productivity.

Thus security and safety managers would want to know about a building control system vulnerability, which could cast a new light on sudden unexplained malfunctions in multiple building systems. If lighting could be affected, a review of the emergency lighting plan might be called for, updating it based on current building occupancy and usage, as well as recently identified potential threats. This aligns with the concept of continuous improvement, something that is a business strategy for many companies. Sometimes only incremental security or safety improvements are called for when risk models change; updating security and safety measures as conditions change over time is prudent.

An Example of Responsible Disclosure

A number of readers have asked for an example of what a vulnerability disclosure looks like. These are often also called security advisories, and I point to an online example that is a security advisory from Cisco that was released in May 2010 and updated in June (see http://tinyurl.com/example-security-advisory). This advisory provides an example of the kind of disclosure content that allows system users and those with related security responsibilities to take appropriate action.

In this case the vulnerabilities found could allow adversaries to easily obtain administrative passwords, thus making it possible for outsiders to take control of a building's most critical control systems. The advisory states, "Successful exploitation of any of these vulnerabilities could result in a malicious user taking complete control over an affected device." The notice also warns that the vulnerabilities are present in the legacy products from the Cisco-acquired company that originally designed the system. The advisory offers several workarounds and common sense configuration settings.

The bugs were discovered during internal testing. In other words, Cisco could have kept the information to itself but did not because that wouldn't be the responsible thing to do. Doing the right thing for the customer doesn't mean doing so just when it bumps up revenue dollars. It means doing it regardless of the short-term impact. In the long term, that strategy is a win-win situation for any well-run and well-intended company.

The details of this particular disclosure reveal another important fact from a bigger picture. The technology helps customers use IT to automate and remotely control tasks that used to require manual procedures. That can provide significant new cost savings for building operators, in part because the product is designed to interact seamlessly with larger power grids. *IT, corporate security, and safety managers take note*: with Smart Grid coming, threat models require updating to include the related new risk scenarios. The Smart Grid actually reduces many risks that are currently unacceptable in our current power infrastructure. Here are three sources of information: the "Smart Grid" topic in Wikipedia (https://en.wikipedia.org/wiki/Smart_grid); the Galvin Electricity Initiative (http://galvinpower.org) for an introduction to many new smart grid concepts; and the Department of Energy's introduction to the rationale behind the Smart Grid initiative (http://energy.gov/oe/downloads/smart-grid-introduction).

One final note: if you don't already have a cross-functional risk committee or risk council, it's a best practice worth considering.

FACING UP TO LOCK-AND-KEY DENIAL

For most physical security programs, "in denial" is the most accurate way to describe the state of lock-and-key management. On day 1, you know the state of *locks*, referring to where they are and how they are keyed, and *keys*, meaning how many there are and who has them—especially master keys. Over time that picture changes, and the state of key controls grows far from what it should be. The larger the organization, the worse the situation gets. It's the "dirty little secret" about physical security programs that is hard to face.

For large organizations, the task is more than daunting; it can seem practically hopeless because maintaining manual lock-and-key programs is not feasible in practice. Add in the fact that there is no way to guarantee that keys won't be copied. Locks and keys are a major vulnerability to internal and external threats. Thus, every year for over two decades I have been asked the question below, especially following the annual ISC West and ASIS shows.

Q: Is there any kind of electronic key system that I can use to supplement or improve the state of my metal lock-and-key program?

A: There are several that you can find at the ISC West and ASIS exhibits.

Intelligent Key Technology

There is more than one kind of intelligent key technology, and I mention two here that take different approaches but have one thing in common: They use intelligent keys to power the locking devices, eliminating the need to change batteries at doors or other access points.

UTC Fire and Security's Supra line of products (part of UTC's acquisition of GE Security) includes electronic key products that can be used to eliminate the use of metal keys. TRACcess is an electronic range of locking and key storage devices powered by the TRACkey (the locking devices themselves require no batteries or other power source). An audit trial of who accessed what and when is maintained through the TRACcess Manager database. Product information can currently be found at http://www.traccessuk.com. Products include the TRAC-Vault intelligent storage device, designed to hold multiple keys or access cards on-site; the TRAC-Padlock designed for outdoor gate and general requirements; and the TRAC-Tube attack-resistant intelligent storage device, which can hold two keys and access cards.

The CyberLock technology from Videx has won multiple product awards, and a client brought it to my attention. The CyberLock technology has two primary hardware components: an electronic key and a replacement lock core for standard locks that contains the electronics for the lock side of the system. The CyberLock cylinder requires no power because it is powered by the CyberKey. The CyberLock requires no network connection because the transaction information is carried back by the CyberKey. A software application collects access history and provides key and keyholder management. It includes an application program interface for integration to access management systems. Videx has even engineered a hardened version of their product that can withstand a taser attack.

Strengthening Key Management

With these kinds of solutions available, every facility and security manager can now significantly improve the state of lock-and-key programs—including management of locking cabinet access. This is an area of convergence (computer intelligence inside physical lock systems) that has been generally neglected for far too long. Regardless of the size of your organization, there is no longer any excuse for having an unintelligent lock-and-key situation. So, do your homework, improve your asset protection profile, and establish a lock-and-key program that you can be proud of.

PRANK—OR BIGGER THREAT?

The incident described in the question below occurred with a high school video system, but similar circumstances could apply to systems in any environment.

> **Q: At Halloween some students taped little black paper witches over a few indoor camera lenses. Later we found motion detection disabled on some cameras. How should we protect the cameras?**
>
> **A:** Camera protection requires a balance of detection and prevention, based on the risk picture.

Camera Attack

During the "paper witch" incident, the assumption at the monitoring desk was that the black camera views meant a partial video outage—probably the intended effect. Having no other information to go on, a service call was requested from the video provider, when of course facility personnel could have quickly and easily removed the taped-up paper witches.

The loss of motion detection was a more serious issue that was not immediately discovered. It turned out to be a result of resetting the affected cameras to factory defaults. The knowledge to do this is available on the Internet. There was no hard evidence available, but the assumption was that the resets were performed when the cameras lenses were covered.

Camera Physical Protection

It's not possible to protect against all possible video loss. A good sledge hammer hit can take out a camera, and unless spare cameras are on hand for immediate replacement, such damage would leave the camera's field of view uncovered for a day or two. The same degree of video loss would occur if a camera lens were spray-painted, unless a replacement lens was on hand. By blocking its view of the target area one way or another, any camera can be defeated temporarily without damaging it at all.

Camera-hardening features should be selected based on the likely threats, as well as cost and aesthetic considerations. One high school mounts its outdoor cameras on high, sturdy poles to safeguard them against physical attacks, including a chain pull attack, whereby students throw a long chain around the camera mount and try to pull the camera down. The same school has a design practice of making sure that each camera is within the field of view of at least one other camera. Camera scene change detection analytics alert the school to camera shaking, as well as to lens blockage by spraying opaque liquids on the camera lenses. It's the combination of the hardening and recorded surveillance measures that were effective in deterring the camera attacks.

In low-risk environments, where camera cables are run in the open without fear of tampering, there can still be accidental damage from maintenance, remodeling work, or even cleaning activity. Video systems can also be subject to technical vulnerabilities; network and hard drive failures are two examples of technical problems that can occur. Thus a combination of video safeguarding measures for *prevention, detection, and response* to video outages should be utilized. The typical manual effort of checking camera views is only partially effective in discovering video problems.

Prevention

Vandal-resistant cameras and camera enclosures are available; these can be installed so that cables and reset controls are not accessible without removing the camera from the wall—something that security screws can make infeasible. Other preventive measures for critical video include putting camera power over Ethernet (PoE) power sources and network switches on an uninterrupted power supply backup and emergency power and using industrially hardened switches for harsh environments.

Lightning rods and lightning surge suppressors are appropriate for outdoor camera installations where lightning risk exists. In high-lightning areas, using fiber optic network cable instead of copper cable can help protect the switching infrastructure.

Running armored conduit and flexible metal conduit connectors is appropriate when cable would otherwise be unsafely exposed. There are many brands of network port locking products that can be used with standard switch and camera network ports in low-risk areas where network cable connections are exposed. Keep in mind that these won't stop a determined attacker from, for example, simply cutting the cable. They can, however, be effective at keeping people from trying to "borrow" a network connection port or from unplugging a cable "just for fun."

Detection

There are both camera-based and server-based analytics for camera scene change detection, which can detect a range of problems, not just camera repositioning or view blocking. Many network cameras also have tamper alarms.

Using network monitoring software to run ping checks on network cameras will not always detect when cameras are not functioning, but it will detect when they are not reachable via the network. Enabling a camera to send syslog events to a syslog server (most IT departments run or can run a syslog server) will provide event messages indicating camera restarts, failed logon attempts, and other events that can indicate isolated and recurring problems. Other network monitoring tools can be used to watch and report when the amount of video traffic on a network path drops below a level that would indicate video transmission loss.

Response

Quite a few network cameras have two-way audio capability, and some include built-in motion detection and can activate a light-emitting diode and play a prerecorded audio file when motion is detected. An officer receiving a camera-related alarm can use the two-way audio capability to warn away trespassers or intruders, whether they intend to harm the cameras or are planning vandalism or theft.

Whether you have risk of prankster activities or worse, be sure to take appropriate measures to safeguard your video system's full-time effectiveness.

WHEELS OR ELECTRONS?

This is the convergence question that you must ask yourself with regard to supporting your installed technology. *Do you want to roll wheels or send electrons?* This relates to the question below, which is one that I am often asked because my colleagues and I are so insistent upon establishing meaningful monitoring of electronic physical security systems.

Q: Why do you insist that tools be installed for network monitoring as part of every security systems project?

A: Because no networked electronic security system deployment is complete without it.

Case Study Example

For a recent security video deployment, we specified the Solarwinds ORION product (a simple network management protocol (SNMP) monitoring product) for network monitoring. What's Up Gold is another product in common use. On this particular project, when one of the cameras went offline and stopped sending video, ORION sent an email message to our client's network technician. He sent an email note to the integrator and copied me, asking them to come out and service the camera. Neither the technician nor the systems integrator is in the same city where the camera resides.

I called the technician and suggested that first he use ORION to cycle the network port that the camera is connected to; this would cycle the power to the camera (it's a PoE installation). He did so, and the camera started sending video again. Not only did the integrator avoid rolling a service truck in a 4-h service call, the restoration of video took only 10 min.

This reminds me to say that network personnel track the uptime records of their systems and devices. Is that something you are doing with your electronic security systems? (It's an important metric, and probably a subject for a future column.)

Follow-Up

We were smart enough not to classify the incident as resolved, because while we did restore the video we didn't know what had caused the problem. This is where having a network baseline profile comes in handy. For this particular project we required that the systems integrator get a baseline picture of the network before putting cameras and servers on it.

This is a 15-min step that can be done using the free Wireshark tool or an equivalent. Once you have captured 5 min of network traffic, you can analyze the traffic for evidence of existing network problems, which of course should be resolved before putting any equipment onto the network. Once the security equipment is connected to the network and set up, you take another snapshot and do a comparison.

Following up on the camera incident, we've stepped up the monitoring of network traffic; if it occurs again we'll have a better picture of what was going on with the network at the time, and we can compare that with the original baseline picture.

Getting the Full Picture

You should also examine the workstation and server logs for network-related messages. No deployment should be considered sufficiently examined without this step. For example, we once found this printer-related message on a workstation computer connected to a video network:

> Bonjour Service. Client application bug: DNSServiceResolve(Kodak ESP7200+1630_smb_tcp.local.) active for over two minutes. This places considerable burden on the network.

Such problems must be resolved before the deployment can be considered fully operational.

Many Reasons for Monitoring

The printer-related message also illustrates another reason for instituting network monitoring. People can innocently connect computers and office equipment to a network, permanently or temporarily, and introduce problems without being aware of it. All kinds of things can happen—this is just one example.

Properly qualifying the condition of the network is an important part of deploying networked security systems. Following that, keeping an eye on the network condition is an ongoing requirement. And whenever possible, send electrons over rolling wheels.

A PASSION FOR SIMPLE NETWORK MANAGEMENT

As you may already know, SNMP actually stands for "simple network management protocol." But I can't help having a passion for it. SNMP is one of the protocols used by the network tool I mentioned in the previous section. I am often asked the following question about this network monitoring passion of mine.

Q: Why do you make such a big deal about the SNMP support of leading-name products?

A: Because the opposite of simple is complex, and that's what supporting medium- and large-scale networked security systems can be if you can't use SNMP.

I know the protocol's name is intended to convey that the protocol is simple but I like pointing out that its use can help make your technology deployment and support work simple, too.

When I'm talking to vendors, I am looking specifically for SNMP version 3 support. SNMP version 3 added security and remote configuration management elements to the protocol. I ask vendors about the SNMP support of their products partly because I want to see what the vendor's response to the question is. If they dance around it or try to minimize the value of SNMP, that tells me that they are at least slightly out of touch with the network environment of today's and tomorrow's deployments. Six years ago, if you had SNMP support in your security system product, hardly any customer was likely to use it—maybe none. That's not the case today.

The most common vendor comment I hear about not supporting SNMP is that "customers aren't asking for it." Supposedly Henry Ford once said, "If I'd asked customers what they wanted, they would have said a faster horse." Once customers started seeing horseless carriages, however, they did start asking for them. The difference is that Henry Ford's company led the industry at that time, and other companies followed. By the way, leading network cameras (such as those from Axis, Bosch, and Pelco) already do support SNMP version 3.

It Means More Than You Think
Another reason I ask about SNMP support is because I need to estimate how much time it will take to qualify a product as network-ready, and how much trouble it may be to support it in the network environment. If there is no SNMP support, or if only SNMP version 1 is implemented, I know we have some product testing to do. A colleague's recent experience makes the point. He scanned a security systems network using NMAP, a product name that stands for "network mapper." It's a commonly used open-source tool for network exploration and security auditing.

The NMAP scan took *all* of the name-brand megapixel cameras offline. (I'll call them "brand X" cameras.) They all had to be manually restarted. When I looked in the brand X camera data sheets and architecture and engineering specs, I saw five network protocols listed, *but not SNMP*. It is not supported. Of course, that was no surprise after the scanning debacle.

This is an example of why my colleagues and I want to see exactly what version of SNMP is supported. We also want to see instructions for setting up SNMP version 3 in the product's installation guide. The lack of these is a red flag that trouble may be ahead.

When brand X's cameras go onto the network, the network security personnel have to put the cameras' Internet protocol addresses on the exception list of their network security scanning software. Their cameras are especially vulnerable, which means that specific kinds of network monitoring are required to catch and respond to network traffic that could disable the cameras—and we're talking about protecting the device from standards-based network traffic. Now consider what protection is needed against malicious network traffic, to which the cameras are seriously vulnerable in many ways. That means network security to ensure that the cameras stay online becomes a very high priority. What network manager would want that kind of product on his or her network? None who I know.

These and other precautions all add time and cost to the deployment. We want to go in the other direction. We want to strengthen our deployments, simplify their support, and include our security system devices in the network monitoring plan. Don't you?

LOG ME IN, SCOTTY!

I recently heard a security system end user describe a situation where a video camera had stopped transmitting video, and when she went to check the camera's settings, the password she had been using no longer worked. The installer had changed the camera passwords and had failed to notify her. She couldn't answer to her boss as to the condition of the cameras. It was unsettling to think that camera settings may have changed without her knowledge.

Per many end user reports, the state of password management for security systems and devices ranges from good to not good to very bad. Most often it's not good, and the question below is, unfortunately, a common situation.

> **Q: I just learned that the company who maintains our security systems uses the same field technician logons on all systems and devices installed by the company. The logons for our system and devices are the same as the logons of other customers all around our city. The company has had personnel changes over the past few years, yet I was told that our passwords (and those of their other customers) were not changed. They also have been using a subscription-based remote access management service to remotely access our systems, which also uses common passwords. We didn't know that this access was even in place. It violates company policy here. All of this means that other customers know the logons to our systems and devices, as well as potential disgruntled employees of the company and their other customers. Am I wrong to be seriously concerned about this?**

A: You are very right to be concerned about this from many perspectives. When you realize that a single inappropriate video clip appearing on YouTube could be a job-ending event, it's not only a cause for concern but a cause for immediate action.

Company-wide installer passwords for customer installations was a security and control systems vulnerability long before the arrival of the Internet, but in earlier times it required a physical presence in a control room or equipment closet to accomplish system access. Now that our systems and devices are networked, and because those networks are much less secure than most believe, it is a very serious vulnerability.

In addition, my colleagues and I commonly find security system servers and devices, including cameras, accessible from conference room network connections. We have been able to call up cameras interfaces in browsers and view video without a password being required on more occasions than you might imagine.

Do You Know Where Your Passwords Are?

Many security practitioners are in a situation where they cannot provide acceptable answers to one or more of these questions:

- Who is responsible for managing passwords for security systems and devices?
- Where is the record of authorized users kept?
- Are there emergency logons in place, stored in an appropriate location that is recorded in a disaster recovery/business continuity plan?
- Who audits password management?
- Are device and server passwords sent "in the clear" or over a secure network connection?
- How frequently are password audits performed?
- What are the password audit criteria (such as a factory default password check or a written password management policy or procedure)?
- Are services hosted by a third party used to provide remote access?
- Is the default state for remote access "disabled" until an actual need to use it arises?
- Do password management and remote access practices comply with IT policy on managing access to the organization's critical systems?
- Where is device authentication (whereby devices must authenticate themselves to be allowed on the network) on the IT network technology roadmap, and at what point will that be applied to security system devices?

Increasing Number of System and Device Logons

As networked cameras and card readers proliferate, the number of system and device logons is increasing dramatically. Even small and medium-size organizations can have a significant number of logons to manage. For example, in a 50-camera system with live monitoring, each camera should have separate logons for setup and maintenance, viewing, camera control (such as pan-tilt-zoom (PTZ) control), and administration (such as adding and deleting users and adjusting system settings). Password management can easily become lax without specific policy to specify it, appropriate network security to enforce it, and standard practice to maintain it.

Access Management

Existing network access management technology can be put to good use for protecting physical security systems, and leading companies have extended their good information security practices to cover networked physical security systems. Standalone deployments can benefit from good network security practices, as well, and they are always feasible to implement.

COSTLY CABLE KINKS

Thus today we have a situation where many security system integrators install network cable without following standard network cabling practice. Finding kinked or stretched cables is not that uncommon. Category 5 and 6 network cable can't be handled in the same manner as other types of cable, and it can easily be damaged by handling that wouldn't affect other cable types. The weight of cable bundles in large control panels or equipment racks often strains the network cables at their connectors. Solid copper wires wrapped around terminal screws can generally withstand much more weight than a standard network cable and its connector, yet many installers handle both types of cable the same way. In general, installers believe that a network cable either works or doesn't. That's not the case. A network cable can be faulty and still seem to be "working," as discussed below. This question arose from such a situation.

> **Q: We were having trouble where a few of our cameras would go offline once a week or so. Cycling the camera's network port (a PoE port) rebooted the camera, but the camera would go offline again some weeks later. The consultant asked the integrator to come in and check the network cable with a cable testing device. Some of the cable failed the test, was replaced, and the cameras using that cable no longer went offline. Our IT director hit the ceiling when he learned of this and shouted, "You mean they didn't certify the cable when they installed it?" What kind of certification is he talking about? Why could we view and record video if the cable was bad?**
>
> **A:** The certification is not a training certification, but a certification of the cable itself using test equipment. The following explanation is paraphrased from Wikipedia. In copper twisted pair wire networks, copper cable certification is achieved through a thorough series of tests in accordance with

Telecommunications Industry Association (TIA) or International Organization for Standardization (ISO) standards. These tests are done using a certification-testing tool, which provides "pass" or "fail" information for each test. Certification is primarily done by installation contractors. It is this certification that allows the contractors to warranty their work.

I have talked to installers who "verify" their cabling by seeing whether video gets transmitted over the network. If they can open a browser on a laptop and get a web page with video from the camera, they assume that all is okay. Yet it may not be.

On a 10-/100-/1000-Mbps network a poor cable can cause the lower speeds to be negotiated between equipment. The network will be "working," but not at its intended bandwidth. That may not matter much for some access control systems, which generate small amounts of network traffic most of the time, but it can have a critical impact on video systems.

In 2002 the Fiber Optic Association reported, "…as much as 80–90% of all Cat 5 cabling was improperly installed and would not provide the rated performance." Contractors have told us that 40% of their Cat 6 installations pass certification tests. Untwist the wires too much at a connection or remove too much jacket and the cable may fail crosstalk testing. Pull it too hard (only 25 pounds tension allowed!) or kink it and [you] lose the performance you paid for.

A cable can be faulty and still transmit data because the network switches can buffer data and retransmit packets that don't get through on the first attempt. This can mask a faulty cable.

Good network cabling practice must be followed, and that includes the practice of cable certification. A cable certification report should be part of the deployment documentation for any networked security system project.

Certifying Cable

Most security system technicians install and service networks without sufficient training in networking design, installation, and management. They don't certify the network cable they install. On the other hand, I know of several security integrators who subcontract their large network cable installations to companies who specialize in that work. Their subcontractors use cable testing equipment and provide them with a cable test report certifying that the cable installation is sound. Their own technicians also certify the cable work that they perform on smaller projects.

While network test equipment exists in the $4000 to $12,000 range, a good network cable tester can be had for about $500, like the one you can see in these two YouTube videos: http://tinyurl.com/certifier-demo-part-one and http://tinyurl.com/certifier-demo-part-two/.

It is worth mentioning that there are also cable testers that show the PoE power draw of installed equipment, which can be used to determine the total draw on a PoE switch. A complete examination of cable testing equipment is beyond the scope of this column, as is a discussion of cabling infrastructure standards and training. But I'd be remiss in not mentioning BICSI (www.bicsi.org), which serves more than 23,000 IT system professionals, including designers, installers, and technicians who provide the fundamental infrastructure for telecommunications, audio/video, life safety, and automation systems.

TECH PROJECTS UNDERMINED BY POOR TRAINING AND DOCUMENTATION

Today's physical security devices and systems require a significant amount of configuration compared with the technologies of a couple of decades ago. Although cameras and other devices can be dead on arrival and hard drives can fail, those are not the common causes of ongoing device and system problems.

Poor configuration by unqualified technicians is a common factor in persisting system problems, as was the situation underlying this reader's question:

> **Q: What ever happened to troubleshooting and root cause analysis? My company's engineers do it all the time. It seems like my security integrator knows only two problem-solving actions: reboot and replace.**
>
> **A:** Unfortunately, this is a too-common situation with multiple contributing factors, including end users who shortchange their own security projects by failing to specify and insist on two things: (1) training and certification requirements for integrator project personnel; and (2) fully complete, as-built documentation and detailed trouble-shooting documentation.

The Training and Experience Factor

Historically, a high percentage of projects with persistent troubles have personnel who are underqualified in terms of experience and training, including project management and technical training. Many of the project team members had no product or general technical training or certification. Of the remaining team members, none had any training or certification participation beyond 2008, and that training was probably written several years earlier. Obviously, much has happened in terms of technology advancement since then.

The Security Industry Association (www.siaonline.org) has an excellent Certification Security Project Manager program, based on the Project Management Institute's Project Management Body of Knowledge, but it is specifically created for managing electronic physical security technology deployment projects. Check the website's Education & Training section to obtain current information.

Troubleshooting

Most technicians in nonsecurity industries get formal training in trouble-shooting as part of their education. It's not a product-specific thing but a process to apply to a problem situation. Here is one example. Tooling University LLC (www.toolingu.com), an online educational company of the Society of Manufacturing Engineers, provides a course called "Troubleshooting: Taking Corrective Actions" (http://bit.ly/toolingu-troubleshooting). The course defines troubleshooting as "a systematic approach to solving problems quickly and efficiently." It often involves a logical process of elimination to identify the true source of a problem, and it attempts to identify the root cause of a problem rather than simply addressing the symptoms. The course also details the importance of documentation in the troubleshooting process.

Troubleshooting skill is developed by applying troubleshooting principals in one's field of work. I have talked to tech personnel who were unaware of the fact that troubleshooting is a defined process that is taught in mechanical, electrical, electronic, and computer engineering schools. Go to Tooling U's Troubleshooting course web page to see the class outline and class objectives.

Documentation is Critical

Documentation is critical to troubleshooting efforts, and that is where fixing troubled security projects can be stopped dead in its tracks. Many security projects have no as-built documentation at all, and some have only physical installation documentation and no records of system setup. Poor or nonexistent as-built documents will cost you time, money, and security.

Rarely does one find a configuration plan, which is a design document that explains how security devices and systems will be configured to achieve their functional and performance objectives. During the acceptance testing process, all the commissioning work is checked against the configuration plan. Without a plan—which is where many security departments are today—acceptance testing is impossible because there is no basis for determining whether devices are set up correctly, and you will not have a starting point to use in managing future settings changes and upgrades.

If you don't know how things are supposed to be set up, how do you know they are set up correctly?

Following Company Policy on Change Management

The configuration plan and initial setup is only step 1. The next aspect is "change management," which is a set of processes and procedures for managing the changes and upgrades to device and system configurations. IT departments usually have a change management (or configuration management) policy document, which describes key requirements that apply to making changes to deployed technology. Many security departments are in violation of these policies and practices, which are developed to ensure the operational success of critical technology.

Needlessly High Costs

When as-built documentation is poor or incomplete, the overall cost of troubleshooting skyrockets because of repeated duplication of efforts. I once observed a 5½ hour service call that started with 3 hour of wire-tracing (the cables were not labeled), an hour of checking software to find what the device and system settings were, and another hour of finding and reading manufacturers' documentation. All this research—which would have been completely unnecessary with proper documentation—was followed by a whopping 15 min of corrective action.

If the documentation was available on-site, it would have resulted in a 30-min service call, and it would have been a lot cheaper; in fact, this particular service call cost the customer more than 10 times what it should have. And because the service technician did not label any wires and did not leave behind a detailed record of the service work, the next technician will probably have to repeat some or all of the research process.

This is not even a worst-case example. A colleague of mine periodically refers to the "$50,000 door," a situation where a $5000 door was replaced 10 times over a period of 5 years because it kept generating nuisance alarms. Once the nuisance alarm rate got too high, the monitoring operators masked the alarm, creating significant security vulnerability.

The door problem was a relatively minor periodic expenditure in the context of a multiyear, multimillion-dollar construction project, and for a long time it went unnoticed. When an audit uncovered the continuing problem, it was permanently fixed for less than $500. The lack of change management and a failure to perform root cause analysis were at the bottom of this hidden problem.

Whether your company's IT department calls it "change management" or "configuration management," don't think of it as an "IT compliance requirement." A more productive view is that it's a fiscal responsibility, a process to ensure the continued reliability of your security systems, and a prime ingredient in job security. (Security personnel jobs were lost as a result of the two problem situations above.)

Your situation might not be as bad as those described above; after all, there are plenty of fully qualified security integrators out there. But without complete as-built documentation that includes device and system configuration information, you can bet you and/or your service providers are spending more on maintaining your technology deployments than you should be.

READ THE RELEASE NOTES!

This reader's question relates to the handling of security system device updates.

Q: We've had a persistent periodic problem with one of our security products, and the integrator's technician called saying that he wanted to install a new release of the software to see if it fixes the problem. The IT person who helps support our deployments asked, "What did the release notes say?" He replied, "I'll find out." Her eyes practically popped out of her head. Why would she have such a strong reaction to his answer? If it's that important, why didn't the technician read the release notes before calling us?

A: It is not surprising that she would be concerned. It has long been standard practice to the review release notes *before* making the decision to install an update. Failing to consult the release notes calls into question the service technician's qualifications.

IT personnel reading this may be surprised that I have written about the topic, and I probably wouldn't have except that I recently encountered two security system deployments where updates had been installed without consulting the release notes. On one hand, I'm sure most security system technicians consider this to be a "Software 101" topic. Yet, looking into this more closely, I found that on a number of projects the release notes were being read, but not closely enough; sometimes they were read only *after* installing the update, and sometimes not at all.

Software and Firmware Release Notes

Most of our security technology today is "intelligent technology," which basically means—from the perspective of this column—that it contains updatable computer code. That code will be firmware or software. (Firmware is code that stays in the memory chip even when the power to the chip is turned off. Software is code that has to be loaded into memory again each time the device is powered up.)

Release notes from the manufacturer should accompany every new version or update to the firmware or software that is released to customers. A release note is usually a text, Word, or HTML document that provides information, usually in bullet lists or numbered notes, about what changed in the software.

Davin Ganroth, Vice President of User Experience for *Covenant Eyes, Inc.*, wrote an article about writing release notes when he couldn't find any published "best practice" on release notes (http://blog.davingranroth.com/2010/03/how-to-write-release-notes/). This is a good reference on what you should find in a release note. If you find that a manufacturer is not providing you with good release notes, please refer them to this article. If you don't, then don't complain the next time you get a bad release note from them!

Reading Release Notes

When troubleshooting a problem, two specific release notes should be studied: the release notes for the current version that's installed, and the release notes for the recommended update. It helps to know whether the problem you are dealing with has already been found, by virtue of its inclusion in the Known Issues section of the current version's release notes. Then look in the update's release notes and see whether you find it listed under "Fixes" or "Corrections." If not, then you should contact the manufacturer to find out if the fix is planned for the next release. If so, then you probably want to wait for the next release since that's the one that is intended to fix the problem.

If the problem you are experiencing is not listed in the "Known Issues" or "Corrections" sections of the release notes, then the prudent action would be to file a trouble ticket with the manufacturer or use whatever official reporting mechanism exists. I mention this because I have found several organizations that don't file reports on product problems, either directly or through their systems integrator. They just wait for the next update to see whether that will fix the problem—a lazy approach that's in no one's best interests.

Confidence is an important factor in customer technology decisions, and release notes can have an impact on this. On one deployment the technician told the customer, "Let's hope this update solves the problem." The customer had serious concerns about the product, and was considering using a different and more expensive product in a deployment that was just starting. In this case, had the technician read the release notes, he could have seen that the problem was listed under "Corrections" and informed the customer. This would have saved the customer needless worry and research.

DETECTING THE GRADUAL LOSS OF VIDEO NETWORK CAPACITY

The arrival of gigabit networks made megapixel security camera deployments much more feasible. However, in spite of network improvements, in some companies the bandwidth available for security video has been shrinking.

> **Q: We recently had a safety incident, and when managers and executives tried viewing the video from their offices or in the field, most video displays were corrupted or would fail. How can this be when nothing changed about the video system?**

A: Remote viewing of video—by which I mean viewing video from outside the security monitoring center—typically uses shared network paths. The problem could be that the business network has less bandwidth available for video than it used to.

Most network video systems are installed with the cameras and recording video servers on dedicated local area networks that provide high-bandwidth connections between cameras and video servers. Security monitoring centers usually have high-bandwidth connections to the video servers or use low-bandwidth video streams for live monitoring consistent with the level of network bandwidth available.

A few video management systems automatically adjust the resolution and frame rate of the viewing video stream based on the size of the image at the viewing end and the available network bandwidth.

For most video systems, remote-view video streams must be configured to match the low levels of bandwidth based on the capacity of network connections.

How Security Video Bandwidth Shrinks

When high-bandwidth networks are first installed or upgraded, there is usually ample network bandwidth to go around. Once the upgraded network infrastructure is in place, however, its use is not static. Over time, the business use of the enterprise network expands, and network traffic increases.

Where plenty of bandwidth was initially available to view a few video streams from anywhere on the network, as business network use increases there may be less available bandwidth for video. Two things can happen: video viewing can degrade or video traffic can interfere with business network traffic. Either condition can result in complaints to the IT department.

When IT Shuts Down Video Networking

Sometimes when video traffic starts causing a problem, video local area networks are disconnected from the enterprise network. This may not be security's fault. IT can make network changes that don't take security video into account. For example, one entire school district was disconnected from its department of education's network because a router at the district offices was misconfigured and allowed video traffic to travel into the department of education's network, creating significant disruption there. In such a situation IT can block video traffic as the first move in getting the business traffic flowing again.

Network configuration or usage changes can unintentionally block video traffic or restrict bandwidth for video without anyone noticing initially. Then, when a security incident occurs and the use of security video ramps up, the problem is suddenly discovered at the worst possible moment.

A significant contributing factor is that the use of remote video viewing is often infrequent, has no regular pattern, and so is not "visible" to IT as normal network traffic. Sometimes network security software will block a flood of video traffic that suddenly appears out of nowhere because it looks like a network attack.

Keeping Video Bandwidth Intact

It is not hard to keep video network bandwidth intact across the network infrastructure.

1. **Document the network requirements**. One video system deployment required more than 25 specific requirements for network protocols and network switch port configurations. Make sure you get this information, as well as calculate the bandwidth requirements for each network path video will travel on, including redundant paths.
2. **Appropriately configure remote views**. If you respect the business by not being wasteful of network bandwidth (and document your approach), IT will respect the network requirements that you provide.
3. **Test and document video network traffic**. Many IT departments use Wireshark or similar free network monitoring software to capture and examine 5 min of video network traffic from a newly deployed security video system. They examine the traffic log to verify and document the acceptable state of the new system. Video-savvy IT departments or security integrators repeat this exercise annually from a good sampling of locations where video viewing is desired. This is information to be shared and evaluated by security and IT.
4. **Document and register the video high-availability requirement with IT security**. Maintaining the integrity of security video traffic a standard part of network security, whose job it is to maintain the confidentiality, integrity, and availability of critical systems.

ONGOING MAINTENANCE FOR OUTDOOR SECURITY CAMERAS

For some years now, there has been an increasing trend of IT departments being given responsibility for electronic security system deployments. This question came from an IT manager, who for the first time was charged with defining the scope of an annual service contract for an outdoor video camera system.

Q: Is our facilities department kidding me when they ask how we're going to keep birds from building nests in our outdoor camera housings?

A: It is no joke that birds, rodents, and insects can all detrimentally affect security video deployments. Cable insulation can make good nesting material for small birds and rodents, and spiders often like to build webs over the camera housing's faceplate. Wasps and bees have also built small nests in fixed camera housings. In the winter, cameras can be a nice place to get warm.

It would be an unlikely situation for an IT department to install computers on outside building walls or on parking lot poles—typical places where outdoor cameras go. So the scope of work involved in ongoing maintenance for outdoor cameras is not the kind of thing most IT departments have had to deal with before.

Ongoing Outdoor Camera Maintenance

Not only do outdoor cameras and housings require inspection and cleaning, but target scene lighting levels must be checked, as well as the possible encroachment of greenery or other obstructions that block the camera's field of view. This is best done by comparing saved images with the current images that the cameras provide. When saving or exporting camera images for review purposes, be sure to note the date and time the image was captured. To support the evaluation of scene lighting, reviews should be done at about the same time of day that the original image was captured. Saving images once each season provides a helpful review library.

Special Considerations

Dirt or dust on a PTZ camera's dome can cause the camera's autofocus function to focus on the dome, blurring the camera's normal image. Light from internal camera infrared illuminators (usually a ring of infrared light-emitting diodes around the camera lens) is reflected back into the camera's sensor even by very light accumulations of dust or dirt on the camera's dome or housing faceplate. Camera images from such cameras should be reviewed regularly to ensure the clarity of the image is sufficient.

Dome Camera Maintenance

The dome of the camera must be cleaned inside and out. These cleaning tips also apply to indoor cameras.

- For a significant amount of dry dirt or sand on the outside of the camera housing or dome, use a dry soft brush to gently brush it clean.
- Alternatively, use a can of compressed air to blow the dust off, being careful not to put the spray nozzle or tube too close to the camera because too much air pressure can push dirt down, creating scratches.
- Use a microfiber cloth to remove any remaining light dirt or dust buildup.
- Remove the dome (or open the dome housing) for access to the inside of the dome.

- Use a microfiber cloth to remove any light dirt or dust buildup.
- If there is a significant accumulation of dirt or grease on the camera dome, wash the dome in warm soapy water and dry it with a microfiber cloth. Do not use paper towels because these may scratch the dome.
- Clean the rest of the camera, inspecting for insect eggs or nests.

Box Camera Maintenance

Outdoor box cameras are typically installed in enclosures designed for them. The enclosures may include a fan and/or heater. Fans and heaters should be tested when the enclosures are cleaned.

- Clean the exterior of the enclosure using a soft brush, air can, or damp cloth, depending on the amount and type of dirt accumulated. For greasy accumulations, use warm soapy water and dry the housing with a microfiber cloth.
- Open the enclosure and inspect for insect eggs, nests, or spider webs. Clean the inside with a soft brush, air can, or damp cloth, taking care not to rub dirt onto the camera itself, especially the lens.
- Check the wiring inside the enclosure to ensure that its insulation is intact and has not deteriorated for any reason; correct any problems found.

Cleaning Camera Lenses

Once in a while you may find that a lens has a fingerprint or other light smudge on it. Use a lens-cleaning pen or cloth because ordinary cleaning materials may scratch the lens or damage any protective coating.

Regardless of the tips above or other guidance you may find, always follow the camera manufacturer's cleaning instructions if any are provided.

THE FACILITY CODE ACCESS CONTROL VULNERABILITY

Many long-time physical security practitioners understand the two purposes of "facility codes" in a card access control system. However, the user manuals and help files of systems that support this feature rarely highlight the risks that can be involved in enabling this feature.

> **Q: I just discovered that card access to our building's data center is being granted to anyone holding a company access card, even though only four people have been assigned access to it. While troubleshooting I discovered that the reader status is "offline." Why is anyone being granted access at all if the card reader is not even communicating with its controller?**

> **A:** The card reader has "facility code mode" enabled, which is a feature whereby the reader grants access to any card containing a facility code that's listed in the reader.

"Facility code mode" is an optional card reader mode that engages when a reader goes offline. One purpose of this mode is to prevent having to prop doors open and revert to manual inspection of access cards to screen entering personnel if a card reader loses its connection to its controller. Facility codes are programmed into readers at the factory or by the customer's access control system. They allow an offline reader to read and validate the facility code portion of a card's encoded data to identify a valid company access card and grant access, even though the reader cannot validate all of the card's encoded data. For example, during peak access hours an offline reader at an employee entrance can grant access to any valid company card, even though it can't validate individual cards against their assigned access privileges.

The question above turned out to be a case where facility code mode was enabled for the facility's data center to ensure that emergency access to the room could be obtained even if the card reader went offline. At some point, however, the IT department stopped monitoring access on a real-time basis and began reviewing access history quarterly. Thus the "offline reader" alarm message was not seen for just over 2 months, during which time access to the room was available to any cardholder!

What is a Facility Code?

A facility code is a number encoded on access cards that is intended to represent a specific protected premises (facility or building). Not all card formats support a facility code, but the most common card data format in use today does support it, the industry's original open (i.e., nonproprietary) format: the 26-bit format. The 26-bit format has two data fields, a facility code (8 bits) and a card number (16 bits), plus two parity bits. Thus the facility code number can be a number between 0 and 255, and the card number can be between 0 and 65,535.

Dealing with Duplicate Card Numbers

With only 65,535 card numbers available across the cards of all customers using the 26-bit card data format, duplicate card numbers are inevitable. Thus the first purpose of the facility code was to allow customers in close proximity to each other to differentiate their set of cards from another customer's cards. To minimize the occurrence of duplicates, each manufacturer would ideally try to manage the facility numbers it issued to various customers in a specific area. A card with a facility code not matching those used by that specific customer would be denied access, typically generating "access denied—wrong facility code" messages.

Facility Code Vulnerability

One reason that many organizations have switched to smart cards or to cards with a much larger card data format is to reduce or eliminate the likelihood of outsiders having duplicate cards.

Enabling facility code mode for selected readers constitutes a security vulnerability, so it is important to monitor a reader's online status in real time, with offline status notifications going to appropriate personnel. If a reader's facility code mode is enabled on a door where logged card access control is mandated by regulatory requirements, card readers that can buffer offline transactions are required so that access granted by an offline reader can be logged.

Understanding what card format your organization uses and determining whether facility code mode is enabled for any readers is important. If a review of access transactions shows that access has been granted or denied to someone who claims not to have presented a card at that time, realize that the transaction may be from an outsider's card with duplicate card data. Disable access for that card (but continue tracking its use) and reissue a new card in its place.

CAUGHT ON VIDEO: TREES STEALING VIDEO DISK STORAGE

As any technologist knows, changes to the inputs of a system can affect the outputs. When system outputs deviate from what is expected, a key question is; How did the inputs change?

> **Q: Eight months ago we put in an outdoor megapixel camera security video system and were getting more than 30 days of storage. Now we're down to 10 days—but we haven't changed any of the camera or system settings. How can this be?**
>
> **A:** It is likely that trees and other greenery are the culprits affecting the rate of motion-based recording.

Whenever motion-based or other analytic-based recording is used, it is important to remember that the recording is based on conditions in the target environment, and if the target environment changes, so can the amount of recording. That is what happened in this case—the greenery grew outside the areas of the camera's field of view that were being excluded from motion detection.

Motion-Based Recording

When motion-based recording is set up, *motion masking* is often used, whereby rectangular or polygonal areas of the image are marked for exclusion so that motion in those areas will not trigger recording. This is commonly done for trees and shrubbery, so leaves and branches moved by the wind don't trigger recording. Over time, however, the trees or shrubbery grow and can extend beyond masked areas in camera views. In some environments this can increase the amount of recording from a low rate (such as 20%) to a high rate (like 80%).

Detecting Motion

Most video-based motion detection is based on the amount of pixel change in an area of the image. Based on how the motion sensitivity is set, when most or all of the pixels change enough, it's considered motion. So, things that we don't normally think of as moving objects, such as slightly overgrown grass or the dark shadow of a cloud passing over a sidewalk, can trigger recording.

This is why video cameras with motion detection settings, or video management systems using server-based motion analytics, need to have their cameras' fields of view inspected for changes at least quarterly. Seasonal changes in cloud patterns, the growth of vegetation beyond motion-exclusion mask areas, and changes to facility lighting can all impact the amount of recording that takes place unless such sources of "motion" are identified and appropriate compensation is applied using either masking or motion sensitivity settings.

Some Motion Sources Can't Be Masked

Some sources of continuous or recurring motion at the far end of a camera's field of view can't be masked without also masking areas closer to the camera, where the intended target objects or people will be found. Sometimes this can be remedied by moving the location of the camera, but not always. Sometimes other means of motion detection, such as dual-technology passive infrared/microwave motion detection technology can be applied effectively, connecting the detector output signals to the camera alarm input contacts to trigger recording. It can take a bit of study and field testing to identify all the motion detection factors involved and to get things working optimally.

Calculating Storage Requirements

Most video system vendors provide storage calculators that use a percentage factor for the amount of time the camera will actually be recording. Scheduled recording is a fixed factor that is easy to take into account: 12h of recording each day is 50%. When motion-based recording is involved, don't just take a wild guess.

Is there is high motion as employees arrive and depart for work? Add up the rush hour times (start of business hours, lunchtime, and end of business hours) and consider them 100% motion. Add two more hours of 100% recording for sunrise and sunset, since during those times shadows and lighting level changes can be interpreted as motion by the camera. If trees are in the picture, will the wind blow the leaves around on the ground during the autumn? How many days of rain or snow will there be? Factor those in, as well. A little bit of math can be required work before you have the right numbers to enter into the storage calculator, but by fully taking into account the motion factors, you can get a more accurate assessment of storage requirements.

Configuring Motion Detection

In addition to taking into account motion when figuring storage requirements, it should also be considered when setting up motion detection for each camera. For example, it is not necessarily a safe assumption that greenery will always be trimmed back to match the camera motion-exclusion masks. Where feasible, vegetation motion masks should be designed to accept a season's worth of vegetation growth, something that may be discernible from earlier video recordings or site photographs or by talking to the facilities or real estate employees who maintain the greenery. Grass-cutting may be curtailed during rainy times, so it may be prudent to consider taller grass levels when setting the sensitivity for grassy areas in windy environments.

A little more thought than is typically given to motion-based recording can make a significant difference in how well the system meets its video storage retention period requirements.

Index